THIS PAGE INTENTIONALLY LEFT BLANK

THIS PAGE INTENTIONALLY LEFT BLANK

George Frideric Handel

Agrippina

OPERA STUDY GUIDE

WITH

LIBRETTO

OPERA CLASSICS LIBRARY™SERIES

Edited by Burton D. Fisher
Principal lecturer, *Opera Journeys Lecture Series*

Opera Journeys™ Publishing   /   Boca Raton, Florida

WEBSITE: www.operajourneys.com   E MAIL: operaj@bellsouth.net

Contents

Opera Journeys™ Mini Guide Series

Opera Classics Library™ Series

Opera Journeys™ Libretto Series

A History of Opera:

Milestones and Metamorphoses

Mozart's Da Ponte Operas

PUCCINI COMPANION

Verdi Companion: 27 Opera Study Guide

<u>*Over 125 GUIDES & LIBRETTI AVAILABLE: Print or Ebook*</u>

•The Abduction from the Seraglio •Adriana Lecouvreur •L'Africaine •Aida
•Andrea Chénier •Anna Bolena •Ariadne auf Naxos •Armida •Attila
•The Ballad of Baby Doe •The Barber of Seville •Duke Bluebeard's Castle
•La Bohème •Boris Godunov •Candide •Capriccio •Carmen
•Cavalleria Rusticana •Cendrillon •La Cenerentola •La Clemenza di Tito
•Le Comte Ory •Così fan tutte •The Crucible •La Damnation de Faust
•The Death of Klinghoffer •Doctor Atomic •Don Carlo •Don Giovanni
•Don Pasquale •La Donna del Lago •The Elixir of Love •Elektra •Ernani
•Eugene Onegin •Exploring Wagner's Ring •Falstaff •La Fanciulla del West
•Faust •La Fille du Régiment •Fidelio •Die Fledermaus •The Flying Dutchman
•Die Frau ohne Schatten •Der Freischütz •Gianni Schicchi •La Gioconda
•Hamlet •Hansel and Gretel •Henry VIII •Iolanta •L'Italiana in Algeri
•Les Huguenots •Iphigénie en Tauride •Julius Caesar •Lakmé •Lohengrin
•Lucia di Lammermoor •Macbeth •Madama Butterfly •The Magic Flute
•The Makropolis Case •Manon •Manon Lescaut •Maria Stuarda
•The Marriage of Figaro •A Masked Ball •Die Meistersinger •The Mikado
•Nabucco •Nixon in China •Norma •Of Mice and Men •Orfeo ed Euridice
•Otello •I Pagliacci •Parsifal •The Pearl Fishers •Pelléas et Mélisande
•Porgy and Bess •Prince Igor •I Puritani •The Queen of Spades
•The Rake's Progress •The Rape of Lucretia •The Rhinegold •Rigoletto
•The Ring of the Nibelung •Roberto Devereaux •Rodalinda •Roméo et Juliette
•La Rondine •Der Rosenkavalier •Rusalka •Salome •Samson and Delilah
•Show Boat •Siegfried •Simon Boccanegra •La Sonnambula •Suor Angelica
•Susannah •Il Tabarro •The Tales of Hoffmann •Tannhäuser •Thaïs •Tosca
•La Traviata •Tristan and Isolde •Il Trittico •Les Troyens •Il Trovatore
•Turandot •The Valkyrie •Werther •West Side Story •Wozzeck

WWW.OPERAJOURNEYS.COM

a Prelude....

OPERA CLASSICS LIBRARY's
Agrippina
STUDY GUIDE WITH LIBRETTO

Agrippina's scenario deals with fictional intrigues involving sex and power politics in Rome around 50 A.D. The opera traces the schemes and ambitions of the Machiavellian-style Agrippina, Emperor Claudius's fourth wife, sister of the infamous Caligula, and mother of Nero, a son from a previous marriage.

Agrippina is considered Handel's first operatic masterpiece, primarily because the score possesses a freshness of musical invention, together with musical characterizations that are subtle and vividly portrayed.

The opera receives its true place among Handel's masterpieces, its popularity increasing as the Baroque revival continues into the twenty-first century.

OPERA CLASSICS LIBRARY explores the greatness of Handel's *Agrippina.* The *Commentary and Analysis* deals with the opera's genesis, biographical and chronological elements, and its premiere and performance history.

The text also contains a *Brief Story Synopsis, Principal Characters,* and a *Story Narrative with Music Highlight Examples.* In addition, the text includes a *Dictionary of Opera and Musical Terms.*

The *Libretto* provides the Itlain-English translation in parallel, a side-by-side format.

The opera art form is the sum of many artistic expressions: theatrical drama, music, scenery, poetry, dance, acting and gesture. In opera, the music composer who is the dramatist; he applies the emotive power of his music and the kinetic intensity of the prose to provide powerful theater, an impact on one's sensibilities that can reach into the very depths of the human soul.

Burton D. Fisher
Editor
OPERA CLASSICS LIBRARY

Agrippina

Drama per musica in Italian in three acts

Music
by
George Frideric Handel

Libretto by
Vincenzo Grimani

Premiere: Venice, Teatro San Giovanni Gristostomo

December 1709

Commentary and Analysis

George Frideric Handel (1685 — 1759) was born in Halle, Saxony, Germany; he died in London, at the age of 74. Handel left a huge legacy of musical compositions, highlighted by volumes of sacred and secular oratorios, and a prolific archive of operas.

Handel began his career studying law, but soon after realizing his exceptional musical talents he developed into an accomplished organist and violinist. At the age of 21, after a brief assignment as a kapellmeister in Hanover, Handel visited London where he found a raging appetite for Italian opera; he remained in London after embarking on a thirty-year career of composing operas. Handel's operas endeared him to the English, and he became their most celebrated musician; Queen Anne appointed him court composer, after which he became artistic director of the newly founded Royal Academy of Music.

Controversy continually surrounded Handel's eccentric character: he was resented as a foreigner; reputed to have been a cruel musical tyrant; envied as a pet of the nobility — and he was despised for his ostensibly boorish manners.

In the end, Handel's popularity and success generated a host of professional envies and jealousies. His enemies gathered around the powerful Earl of Burlington, who in turn imported Giovanni Maria Bononcini, a celebrated opera composer. But after the huge success of Handel's *Ottone* (1723), the heated music war ended with his rivals retiring into permanent retreat. Shortly thereafter, Handel became an English citizen.

Some of Handel's 40 plus operas are: *Almira* (1705), *Rodrigo* (1707), *Agrippina* (1709), *Rinaldo* (1711), *Radamisto* (1720), *Acis and Galatea* (1720), *Floridante* (1721), *Giulio Cesare* (1723), *Tamerlano* (1724), *Rodelinda* (1725), *Scipione* (1726), *Admeto* (1727), *Siroe* (1728), *Partenope* (1730), *Poro* (1731), *Ezio* (1732), *Arianna* (1734), *Atalanta* (1736), *Berenice* (1737), *Faramondo* (1738), *Serse* (1738), *Imeneo* (1740), and *Deidemia* (1741).

Opera seria was the genre of eighteenth-century opera — literally translated as "serious opera"; it was intended to represent musico-dramatic recreations of Greek tragedy, myth, and ancient history — noble, heroic, or tragic settings in which the moral dilemmas of protagonists generally resolved happily, and with due reward for rectitude.

But as the mid-eighteenth century unfolded, the popularity of the opera seria declined and audiences began to consider the genre excessively stilted and formal, and lacking enough dramatic interest to sustain appeal. There were opponents who even considered the opera seria an irrational form of theatrical entertainment, however, much of its demise was attributable to the high cost of mounting opera productions and the exorbitant fees demanded by the castrati and prima donna singers.

The opera seria had become the object of scorn and derision. In 1728, John Christoph Pepusch's *The Beggar's Opera* blatantly lampooned the genre; the satire had the air of a serious opera but its underlying themes were the antithesis of the noble ambience of the opera seria. In the end, Pepusch's opera became a satire about beggars, its setting surrounded by thieves, prostitutes, and criminals, with loose language laced with vulgarity as it ridiculed the Italian opera seria by skillfully adapting popular songs by other composers of the period.

Handel abandoned the opera seria after *Imeneo* (1740) and *Deidamia* (1741) failed to excite the London public's imagination. He proceeded to reinvent himself by developing, innovating, and mastering the English oratorio — narrative choral works strikingly different in format than the theatrical intensity of the opera seria.

Despite the shift to a new genre, Handel's musical compositions — both opera seria and oratorio — possessed highly charged dramatic situations, with profound psychological insight in their characterizations.

Ultimately, Handel earned the honor as the most instinctively musical theater composer during the period between Monteverdi and Mozart.

During the seventeenth century, Claudio Monteverdi, acclaimed for the *L'incoronazione di Poppea* (1642), became one of the opera art form's most significant pioneers. Specifically, Monteverdi innovated the "aria" — a air, or song inserted into the musical scenario to add more intense emotive expressiveness.

Henry Purcell's opera, *Dido and Aeneas* (about 1689), became an innovative landmark of the lyric theater; it emphasized the integration of music and prose into a single organic unity. Christoph Willibald Gluck introduced transformations and reforms that established the lyric theater as the quintessential means to artistically express human emotions and passions; in Gluck's *Orfeo ed Euridice* (1762) and *Alceste* (1767), the composer succeeded in expressing profound dramatic truth through music possessing lofty sentiment and feeling.

Most of the Baroque operas of the opera seria genre were composed in the Italian style by foreigners: Handel was a Saxon who composed Italian-style opera for English audiences; Gluck was a Bavarian composing in Venice before transitioning to Paris.

Pietro Metastasio (1698 —1782) was perhaps the most significant craftsman of post-Florentine Camerata opera: an Italian dramatist, poet and librettist, and prolific author of opera texts, and a writer of poetic dramas based upon classical and Biblical themes; Metastasio's texts would be set to music by an entire generations of opera composers — Handel, Gluck, and later, Haydn and Mozart.

Metastasio's flowery prose was saturated with intricate plots and grandiose climaxes, all appealing strongly to the spectacle-minded eighteenth-century audience: opera themes were intended to be based upon classical mythology, which generally superseded historical themes; reason and virtue would triumph over inconstancy and evil; protagonists were to display noble behavior; only aristocratic characters were permitted to mingle with the gods; and outward displays of excessive emotion was forbidden.

Structurally, there were to be only three, tightly written acts in an opera; conclusions were to be happy, as opposed to tragic.

Baroque describes elaborate and heavily ornamented style of art and architecture. The eighteenth-century Baroque opera seria was especially ostentatious, its traditional construction largely a series of arias for solo singers, very few concerted numbers, a limited use of chorus, and in most instances, the use of intricate stage machinery.

Although opera seria scenarios strove for dramatic perfection and cohesion, they remained "showcases" and "showpieces" for virtuoso aria singers to exhibit their talents. The Italian castrati singers had become the modern equivalent of film stars — the superstars that audiences came to hear, and no other element, whether plot, chorus, or orchestra, could compete with their stature and popularity.

Recitative describes dialogue that carries the action and storyline; it could be either instrumentally accompanied or unaccompanied. The aria became the vehicle for introspection — the medium from which the characters expressed emotion and passion. A perfect opera seria represented a combination of plot-carrying recitatives, joined by a host of arias.

In the end, the aria became the primary element of the opera; the opera story was secondary — an opera comprising a concentration of arias led to fierce competition among the virtuoso singing stars.

Allessandro Scarlatti composed sixty-six operas; his great contribution was the "da capo" aria, literally meaning "from the head." The da capo was a structure of A – B – A, the last A strophe often not written out, but directing the singer to return to the beginning. Ultimately, an opera comprised a host of da capo arias, each "song" illustrating a single emotion or sentiment, such as pathos, anger, heroic resolve, or tender love. One aria might express several emotions at once, but a penetrating psychological portrayal of a complex character might demand five or more arias.

Handel's most acclaimed Italian opera seria was *Giulio Cesare in Egitto* (1724); no other Handel opera has been more successful — either in his own day or presently, with each scene of the opera representing a vivid tableau of human emotion and passion. Handel provided the principal characters — Caesar and Cleopatra — with a string of musical gems that serve as multifaceted portraits of the Roman hero and the seductive Egyptian queen — musical inventions that demonstrated Handel's incredible insight into human character.

During the eighteenth century Baroque era, music in the soprano vocal range was sung by castrati — male singers whose sexual organs were removed before puberty in order to preserve and develop a soprano or contralto vocal range; the practice was condoned by the Roman Catholic Church after citing one of St. Paul's epistles in which women were admonished to remain silent in church.

The castrati first appeared in the seventeenth century in church choirs, but soon made their appearance in the flourishing lyric theater that began after the innovations of the early seventeenth-century Florentine Camerata.

The castrato Farinelli (1705 —1782) boasted an unrivaled, superhuman vocal technique, and was idolized like contemporary superstars of stage and screen. But by the early nineteenth century, a more humane age began to condemn the barbarity of the castrato surgery and it very soon became an illegal practice. The last major composers to write roles for castrati were nineteenth-century masters — Rossini and Meyerbeer.

In later years, roles that had been composed for castrati were either transposed for tenors or were adapted by new generations of female singers entering the lyric theater. More recently, many castrati roles have been sung by the new wave of countertenors and male altos — male signers who produced soprano tones without recourse to surgery.

The countertenor is a rare male voice — a vocal cousin of the castrato, with a range falling roughly between the tenor and soprano. The countertenor voice has the range, flexibility, and brilliance of the female voice, but possesses the muscularity of the male voice. Powerfully convincing countertenors — male altos — have emerged in the last quarter century to endow the voice-type with permanency and legitimacy — a tribute to their extraordinary vocal capabilities.

About a decade before *Giulio Cesare,* Handel had achieved wide acclaim for *Agrippina,* a three-act opera seria composed for the 1709–1710 Venice Carnevale season; the opera is widely regarded as Handel's first operatic masterpiece.

Agrippina's scenario deals with fictional intrigues involving sex and power politics in Rome around 50 A.D. The opera traces the schemes and ambitions of the Machiavellian-style Agrippina, Emperor Claudius's fourth wife, sister of the infamous Caligula, and mother of Nero, a son from a previous marriage.

In the opera scenario, Agrippina launches a conspiracy for the downfall of her husband, Emperor Claudius, and as his successor, secure the throne for Nero, her devious, self-centered son. The opera story involves an interplay of sinister characters, highlighted by conflicts involving lust, anti-heroism, and comic situations that approach satire.

Two powerful women dominate the opera story: the commanding, and at times neurotic Agrippina; and the sexually alluring Poppea, who becomes the wry object of erotic obsession of three men. Poppea's adventures contain flashes of deep emotion but approaches farce after Poppea contrives to have Nero exposed to Claudius as an importunate rival, while she hides each of her three inamoratas in her apartment in quick succession.

After Handel composed *Rodrigo* (1707) during his brief sojourn in Italy, he was approached by Cardinal Vincenzo Grimani, a distinguished diplomat and writer of libretti, who also functioned as an unofficial theatrical agent for the Italian royal courts. Grimani had become impressed by Handel and urged him to set his *Agrippina* to music for the 1709–1710 Carnevale season. Grimani's topical political allusions — as well as the comical, amatory character of Emperor Claudius — presumably represented a caricature of Pope Clement XI, a political and diplomatic rival of Grimani. Likewise, the opera's rivalry between Nero and Otho mirrors aspects of the debate over the War of the Spanish Succession, in which Grimani supported the Habsburgs and Pope Clement supported France and Spain.

Grimani's libretto drew heavily upon Tacitus's *Annals and Suetonius' Life of Claudius;* the opera highlighted irony, deception, intrigue, and humorous escapades of the story's well-defined characterizations. Grimani's *Agrippina* addressed the same underlying story as Monteverdi's *L'incoronazione di Poppea* (1642), although Agrippina, the central character, does not appear; all of the main characters, with the sole exception of Claudius's servant Lesbus, are historical.

Cardinal Grimani's witty and skillfull libretto represents a typical Venetian anti-heroic comedy, with the exception of Otho — an entirely serious character that is demonstrated in his Act II lament, "Voi che udite il mio" — perhaps the most tragic moment of the opera.

All the main characters cynically intrigue for their own purposes, but are redeemed by underlying virtues: Agrippina is essentially unselfish, scheming for her son Nero rather than herself.

The opera premiered at the Grimani family-owned theatre in Venice and was a triumphant success: an unprecedented 27 consecutive performances followed, which effectively established Handel's international reputation.

Following contemporary customs, Handel extensively recycled music for *Agrippina* from earlier works, such as music he had recently composed while in Italy — the opera *Roderigo* (1707) and the oratorio *La Resurrezione* (1708) — as well as music composed by Arcangelo Corelli and Jean-Baptiste Lully, among the many.

Castrati — those ubiquitous superstars of the Italian Baroque opera — performed the main male roles of Nero and Narcissus; they would eventually be replaced by countertenors and male altos.

All the characters reflect certain redeeming features; although they primarily express genuine emotion, some found themselves in unwitting comic situations — their situation satirical, but never farcical.

Handel was a supremely gifted musical painter whose descriptive lyricism abounds in the character's emotions and passions.

The early arias reflect his ingenious talent for musical characterization: Nero's "Con saggio tuo consiglio" is composed in a minor key; the music descends on the phrase "il trono ascenderò" ("I will ascend the throne"), which serves to characterize him as weak and irresolute.

Pallas's first aria, "La mia sorte fortunata," contains wide-leaping melodic phrasing that serves to describe him as a bold, heroic figure, which contrasts with his rival Narcissus, whose introspective nature is displayed in the delicate aria that follows, "Volo pronto."

Agrippina's first aria, "L'alma mia," conveys a sense of triumph, Handel's subtle musical phrasing establishing the sheer intensity of her emotional state. She is at her most formidable in the great scene of Act II, "Pensieri, voi mi tormentate" in which her despair leads her to plan a murder.

Poppea's arias are uniformly light and rhythmic. Claudius's short romance, "Vieni O cara" is a gem of the score, his expression of passion for Poppea.

Handel brilliantly combined the force of the text with the emotional color of the music; Grimani's libretto is saturated with irony, which Handel duly captures in the music.

Deception is always in conflict with underlying truth. In Agrippina's Act I aria, "Non ho cor che per amarti," she promises Poppea that deceit will never mar their newfound friendship, while she simultaneously tricks Poppea into destroying Otho's chances for the throne. Handel's music illuminates her deceit, melodically and through minor key modality; its simple, rhythmic accompaniment suggests clarity and honesty.

In Act III, Nero announces that his passion for Poppea has ended, "Come nube che fugge dal vento" is highlighted by a bitter-sweet lyricism that suggests he is deceiving himself.

In Otho's "Coronato il crin," the agitated nature of the music reflects the opposite of the euphoric tone suggested in the text.

*A*grippina is considered Handel's first operatic masterpiece, primarily because the score possesses a freshness of musical invention, together with musical characterizations that are subtle and vividly portrayed.

Handel's operas fell into obscurity until the Baroque revival of the twentieth century. Today, *Agrippina* receives its true place among Handel's masterpieces, its popularity increasing as the Baroque revival continues into the twenty-first century.

Principal Characters in Agrippina

Emperor Claudius (Claudio)	Bass
Agrippina, his wife	Soprano
Nero (Nerone), Agrippina's son	Soprano
Pallas (Pallante), a freedman	Bass
Narcissus (Naarciso), a freedman	Alto
Lesbus (Lesbo), Claudius's servant	Bass
Otho (Ottone), Commander of the Army	Alto
Poppea, a noble lady of the court	Soprano
Juno (Giunone), goddess of love and marriage	Soprano

e

TIME: about 50 A.D.

PLACE: Ancient Rome

Brief Story Synopsis

Agrippina, wife of Emperor Claudius, receives a letter informing her that her husband died in a storm at sea; she proceeds to intrigue in order that her son Nero shall become Claudius's successor.

As Nero is about to ascend the throne, Claudius's servant Lesbus announces that the emperor was saved from death by the valiant Otho, commander of the army. As Otho's reward, Claudius proclaims Otho his successor.

Otho confides to Agrippina that his love for Poppea supersedes his desire for the throne. Claudius is secretly in love with Poppea.

Agrippina creates an intrigue in which Nero will succeed Claudius: she informs Poppea that Otho promised Poppea to Claudius in return for the throne. Poppea becomes furious and vows to avenge Otho's apparent betrayal.

Claudius becomes enraged and revokes his promise of the throne to Otho. Otho becomes devastated and bewildered, and pleads his innocence of any crime.

Poppea suspects Agrippina's duplicity and becomes obsessed to prove Otho's innocence. Otho hides behind the curtains of Poppea's apartment as Nero arrives to press his love for Poppea; as Claudius is about to arrive, she tricks Nero into hiding as well.

Poppea informs Claudius that he had earlier misunderstood her: it was not Ortho but Nero who had ordered her to reject him.

After Claudius pretends to leave, Poppea summons Nero; after believing that Claudius departed, he resumes his passionate wooing of Poppea. But Claudius suddenly appears and angrily dismisses the crestfallen Nero.

Otho emerges from hiding, and Poppea and Otho express their everlasting love for one another.

Nero informs Agrippina that he has decided to renounce love for political ambition.

Claudius learns of Agrippina's duplicity in seeking the throne for Nero and accuses her of treachery.

Agrippina defends her actions by claiming that she intentionally created a ruse: her efforts to secure the throne for Nero had all along been a ploy to safeguard the throne for Claudius. Claudius believes Agrippina.

Claudius announces that Nero and Poppea shall marry; Otho shall have the throne.

However, no one seems to be satisfied with Claudius's decision.

In the spirit of reconciliation, Claudius reverses his proclamation: Poppea and Otho shall marry; Nero shall be his successor.

Claudius summons Juno, goddess of love and marriage, who descends to pronounce a blessing on all.

Story Narrative with Music Highlight Examples

Act 1: Agrippina's private apartments.

Agrippina has received news that her husband, Emperor Claudius, died in a storm at sea. Upon Agrippina's advice, Nero promises to seek the throne as Claudius's rightful successor.

Con saggio tuo consiglio il trono ascenderò ("I shall ascend the throne with the benefit of your wise counsel")

For their support, Agrippina promises love to Pallas and Narcissus, freedmen of the court. She compares the battle for the throne to defeating a storm at sea.

L'alma mia frà le tempeste ritrovar spera il suo porto ("Amidst the tempest, my soul hopes to reach its port")

As Nero is about to ascend the throne, Claudius's servant Lesbus announces that the Emperor was saved from death by the valiant Otho, commander of the army; as Otho's reward, Claudius proclaims him successor to the throne.

Otho confides to Agrippina that his love for Poppea supersedes his desire the throne.

Poppea prays for Otho's love.

Vaghe perle, eletti fiori, adornatemi la fronte! ("Adorn my brow, precious pearls, and choice flowers!")

Claudius reveals his passion for Poppea.

Vieni, oh cara, ch'in lacci stretto ("Come, my dear, to my tight embrace")

Agrippina lied to Poppea: she informed her that Claudius promised the throne to Otho in return for Poppea's love. Agrippina vows to help Poppea avenge Otho's betrayal.

Non hò cor che per armarti ("My heart exists only for your love")

Poppea denounces Otho and vows to avenge his betrayal.

Se giunge un dispetto a' danni del cor ("If Otho deceived me")

Act II: A street in Rome next to the imperial palace, decorated for Claudius's triumph.

Pallas and Narcissus have concluded that Agrippina deceived them into supporting Nero. Otho is nervous about his forthcoming coronation.

Coronato il crin d'alloro io sarò nel campidoglio ("I shall I be on the Capitol, crowned with the laurel wreath")

Agrippina, Nero, and Poppea greet Claudius and celebrate a triumphal chorus: "Di timpani e trombe al suono giulivo" *("To the joyous clamor of trumpets and drums")*

Claudius rebuffs Otho and denounces him as a traitor. Otho is devastated and pleads innocence of any crime. Agrippina, Poppea, and Nero reject him, leaving him bewildered and in despair: "Voi che udite il mio lamento, compatite il mio dolor!" *("You who hear my complaint, share my grief with me")*

Poppea prays for Otho's innocence.

Bella pur nel mio diletto mi sarebbe l'innocenza ("How lovely it would be to find my beloved innocent")"

Otho laments Poppea's betrayal: "Vaghe fonti, che mormorando serpeggiate nel seno all erbe" *("Pretty streams that murmur while the wind blows along your grassy way")*

However, Poppea realizes that she was deceived by Agrippina.

Ingannata una sol volta esser possa, mà non più ("I can be deceived just once, but not more")

Poppea is confident of Otho's innocence and is determined to uncover Agrippina's deceit. She invites Nero to her apartment, hoping to determine if he conspired against Otho.

Nero joyfully accepts the opportunity to pursue Poppea.

Quando invita la donna l'amante ("When a woman invites her lover")

Agrippina is tormented that her scheme for Nero's succession may be uncovered.

Pensieri, voi mi tormentate ("How you torment me")

Agrippina convinces Pallas and Narcissus that Ortho is an enemy of Rome who must be killed.

She also convinces Claudius that if he abdicates in favor of Nero, he will eliminate Otho as a threat to Rome. As Claudius rushes to a rendezvous with Poppea, he promises Agrippina that he will consider proclaiming Nero as emperor.

Agrippina celebrates the victory of her intrigue.

Ogni vento ch'al porto lo spinga ("Whatever wind blows him to port")

Act III: Poppea's apartments.

Poppea launches a scheme to expose Agrippina's deceit and divert Claudius's wrath from Otho, with whom she has now reconciled. Nero proclaims his love for Poppea, unaware that Otho, Poppea's true love, is hiding in her apartment.

Poppea has hidden both Nero and Otho behind curtains and awaits the arrival of Claudius. Poppea informs Claudius that he misunderstood her: that it was not Otho but Nero who betrayed him. She opens the curtains and reveals Nero's presence; Claudius becomes furious and dismisses him.

After Claudius departs, Poppea calls Otho from hiding; both express their everlasting love for one another.

Bel piacere e godere fido amore! ("Pleasure is the joy of sincere love!")

Nero informs Agrippina that his love for Poppea supersedes becoming emperor and renounces his political ambitions: "Come nube che fugge dal vento" *("As a cloud flies from the wind")*.

Claudius accuses Agrippina of treachery. Agrippina claims that her actions were intended to protect her husband and the throne from a rebellion. Claudius accepts her excuse.

Se vuoi pace, oh volto amato ("If you want peace, my handsome lover")

In a spirit of reconciliation, Claudius gives Poppea's hand in marriage to Otho; and the throne to Nero.

He invokes Juno, goddess of love and marriage, who blesses all Rome.

V'accendano le tede i raggi delle stelle ("The starlight kindles our torches")

Libretto

Act I

Agrippina's private apartments

Agrippina:
Nerone, amato figlio; è questo il tempo,
in cui la tua fortuna prender potrai pe'l
crine, ed arrestarla.
Oggi propizio fato la corona de' Cesari ti
porge.
Svelo a te ciò che a tutti è ignoto ancor.
Prendi, leggi! e vedrai, e ciò che la mia
mente dispone a tuo favor poscia saprai.

Nerone:
"Col duolo a cuor e con il pianto al ciglio
questo fogli ti invio, Sovrana Augusta;
di tempestoso mar nel gran periglio
rimase assorta l'aquila latina,
e Claudio, il tuo Consorte,
nell'eccidio comun trovò la morte."
Claudio morì? Che sento?

Agrippina:
Vuoto è il trono del Lazio, e a riempirlo
per te suda mia mente; già maturo
all'impero, del quinto lustro oggi al confin
sei giunto; in questo dì fatal voglio che
Roma cinga il Cesareo allor alla tua
hioma.

Nerone:
Che far degg'io?

Agrippina:
Senti! Occulta quanto sai,
l'alterigia deponi, umil diventa;
va tra le turbe, e con modesto ciglio
ogn'uno accogli; a' poveri dispensa l'or,
che nascosto tieni, commisera il lor stato,
e s'hai nel cuore.
O senso di vendetta o stimolo d'amore,
copri l'un, l'altro cela;
e non fia grave la finzione all'interno;
se vuoi regnar, i tuoi desir correggi,
che al desio di regnar cedon le leggi.

Agrippina:
Nero, my beloved son! This is the
moment for you to seize your fortune,
grab the throne, it awaits you.
Today, destiny is propitious and offers
you the crown of the Caesars.
I tell you what is not known by all.
Here, read! And you shall know my plans
for your future.

Nero: *(reading the document)*
"With sorrow in my heart and tears in my
eyes, regal Augusta, I send you this letter.
The Roman Eagle was in dire peril on the
stormy seas and sunk,
and Claudius, your husband, and the god
we both honor, met his death."
Claudius is dead? What do I hear?

Agrippina:
Lazio's throne is empty, and to replenish
it I think in terms of your future.
You are ripe for empire: you have arrived
today at the threshold of your twenty-
first year. On this fateful day I intend that
Rome shall offer you the imperial laurel.

Nero:
What must I do?

Agrippina:
Listen carefully! Keep you secret, and
put aside your pride and assume humility.
Go amongst the crowds. Greet everyone
with a modest glance; distribute the gold
you hold in secret to the poor, and
sympathize with their lot.
And if your heart suspects revenge, or
love's betrayal, cover one and hide the
other: do not consider inward deception
serious. Reign by controlling your desires,
for laws bow before the desire to rule.

Nerone:
I tuoi saggi consigli ogn'ora mi saran, madre, si scorta.

Nero:
Your sound advice shall always be my guide, mother.

Agrippina:
Vanne, non più tardar! pronto disponi quanto dettò il mio amore; un momento perduto talor di grandi imprese è distruttore.

Agrippina:
Go, delay no longer! Go immediately; and arrange the scheme that my love has hatched. One moment lost can destroy a great undertaking.

Nerone:
Con saggio tuo consiglio il trono ascenderò.
Men Cesare che figlio, te, madre, adorerò.

Nero:
I shall ascend the throne with the benefit of your wise counsel. I shall be less an emperor and more a son.
You, my mother, I shall adore.

Agrippina:
Per così grande impresa tutto si ponga in opra.
Io ben m'accorsi che Narciso e Pallante, sia per genio o interesse, han nella mente un nascosto desio di vincer il mio cor; ciò che sprezzai or con arte s'abbracci.
Olà, venga Pallante!

M'assista arte e frode in questo istante.

Agrippina:
Let all be set in motion for this great work.
I do know that Narcissus and Pallas, whether from inclination or self-interest, harbor hidden desires to conquer my heart; let what I despised be artfully welcomed.
Come, send for Pallas!
(a page obeys her)
May cunning and deceit assist me now.

Agrippina reveals an extremely melancholy attitude.

Pallante:
A' cenni tuoi sovrani ecco il fido Pallante.

(Mesta il bel volto asconde, e pensierosa a me nulla risponde?)
Alla tua legge, Augusta, hai prove del mio cor, e tu ben sai quanto fido egli sia, quanto costante.

Pallas:
Upon your sovereign command, behold your faithful Pallas.
(She sadly hides her lovely face, but lost in thought does not reply to me?)
You have proof, Augusta, of my heart's obedience to your decrees; you know well how faithful it is, and how constant.

Agrippina:
Ah Pallante! Pallante!

Agrippina:
Ah Pallas, Pallas!

Pallante:
E per chi mai Agrippina sospira?
A toglier le tue pene vorrei esser bastante.

Pallas:
Why does Agrippina sigh? If it was in my power, I would ease your suffering.

Agrippina:
Ah Pallante, Pallante!

Agrippina:
Ah Pallas, Pallas!

Pallante:
(Che favellar è questo? ardir, ardire!)
Il tuo Pallante io sono, son quel
ch'alle tue voglie ha pronto il core.

Agrippina:
Il core!

Pallante:
Sì, sì, il cor, o Regina, e con fido cor ciò
che t'aggrada…

Agrippina:
Sì, sì, t'intendo, sì: col cor la spada.

Pallante:
La spada, il braccio, e l'alma.

Agrippina:
Le tue offerte aggradisco.

Pallante:
Ah, se permesso fosse mai di parlar?

Agrippina:
Parla, discopri!

Pallante:
Io temo.

Agrippina:
Non temer. (Arte s'adopri)

Pallante:
È gran tempo ch'io nutro ardor
che mi divora, ma il rispetto…

Agrippina:
Non più! dicesti assai.

Pallante:
Io chieggio dell'ardir, bella, condono.

Agrippina:
Ti basti ch'io t'intesti, e ti perdono;
il dir di più riserba ad altro tempo.
Pallante, a te sia noto ciò che ad ogni altro
è ascoso. È morto Claudio.

Pallas:
(What does this bold gesture signify?)
I am your faithful Pallas, one whose heart
is yours to command.

Agrippina:
Your heart?

Pallas:
Yes, yes, my heart, o queen, and in my
faith I hear whatever pleases you…

Agrippina:
Like your heart, your sword is at my service.

Pallas:
My sword, my arm, my very soul…

Agrippina:
Your loyalty pleases to me.

Pallas:
Ah, if only I could speak my mind!

Agrippina:
Speak then, reveal your thoughts.

Pallas:
I fear to.

Agrippina:
Do not be afraid. (I must be cunning.)

Pallas:
I have long nurtured a love that devours
me, but out of respect…

Agrippina:
No more, you have said enough.

Pallas:
I seek pardon for my love, my fair one.

Agrippina:
I heard, and I have pardoned you. We'll
discuss it at a later time. Pallas, you shall
know that which has been hidden from all
of the others. Claudius is dead.

Pallante:
Claudio!

Pallas:
Claudius?

Agrippina:
Alle milizie, al popolo s'aspetta di stabilir
del successor la sorte; tu vanne al
Campidoglio, i parziali aduna, e all'or che
farò nota, di Cesare la morte, tosto
Nerone acclama.
Se mio figlio è regnante, con Agrippina
regnerà Pallante.

Agrippina:
The fate of his successor will be settled
by the army and the people.
Go to the Capitol, gather our supporters,
and when Caesar's death is made known,
acclaim Nero immediately.
If my son comes to power, Pallas will
reign with Agrippina.

Pallante:
La mia sorte fortunata dalle stelle oggi mi
scende, se vien oggi da te.
Se in te sol, bella adorata, la mia stella mi
risplende, per gloria di mia fé.

Pallas:
Through you, propitious fate descended
today from the stars, through you to me.
Through you, my lovely adored one, my
star shines, glorifying my faithfulness.

Agrippina:
Or che Pallante è vinto si vinca anche
Narciso.
Olà, Narciso chiama!

Ottien chi finger sa quello che brama.

Agrippina:
Now that Pallas is conquered, let's
vanquish Narcissus too.
Ho there, call Narcissus!
(a page departs)
He knows well how to obtain what he wants.

Narciso:
Umile alle tue piante...

Narcissus:
A suppliant stands before you...

Agrippina:
Non più! di occulto arcano chiamo
Narciso a parte;
te solo oggi destino per fabro di
grand'opra,
e alla tua fede confido ciò, che sin ad ora
celai.

Agrippina:
No more! I called Narcissus aside to
impart a dark secret;
Today, I appoint only you to perform a
great deed,
and entrust you with what I have hidden
until now.

Narciso:
Dispor della mia fé sempre potrai.

Narcissus:
You may always rely on my confidence.

Agrippina:
Quali non so per anche sian del tuo cuor i
sensi, a me li scopri.

Agrippina:
Yet I know not what your true feelings
are: reveal them to me!

Narciso:
Ah! Sovrana Agrippina, quel dir io vorrei
non m'è permesso.

Narcissus:
Ah, sovereign Augusta, that which I
would speak is forbidden.

Agrippina:
Tutto ti sia concesso.

Agrippina:
All shall be allowed to you.

Narciso:
Poiché è lecito il dirlo, dirò ch'io t'amo.

Narcissus:
I am free to speak my mind: I love you.

Agrippina:
E tant'oltre t'avanzi?
Supplice alle tue piante chieggio...

Agrippina:
And can you be so bold?
I supplicate myself at your feet...

Agrippina:
Che chiederai?

Agrippina:
What would you ask of me?

Narciso:
Che pietosi ver me rivolgerai.

Narcissus:
That you gaze upon me with pity.

Agrippina:
Sorgi, e a te sia di mia clemenza un dono
ch'il tuo desir intesi, e ti perdono.

Agrippina:
Rise, it is in my clemency that I
comprehend your desires and forgive you.

Narciso:
Or ch'il mio amor tu sai, felice io sono.

Narcissus:
I am happy that you know of my love.

Agrippina:
Quanto chi in te confida, leggi.

Agrippina:
How much I trust you, read and discover

Narciso:
Cieli, che leggo?

Narcissus:
Heavens, what do I read?

Agrippina:
Or fa d'uopo nella man d'Agrippina
d'assicurar lo scettro.
Vanne tosto colà dove raccolto sta il
popolo e soldato;
ivi attendi ch'io scopra la novella fatal,
e allor prudente il nome di Nerone
insinua fra le turbe.
Se al trono il ciel Nerone oggi destina,
Narciso regnerà con Agrippina.

Agrippina:
Now is the moment to ensure that the
scepter remains in Agrippina's hands.
Go straight to where the populace and
soldiers are gathered;
wait there till I have revealed the fateful
news, then subtly introduce the name of
Nero amongst the crowd.
If today heaven allots the throne to Nero.
Narcissus shall reign with Agrippina.

Narciso:
Volo pronto, e lieto il core è presagio di
gioire.
Volarò da loco a loco sovra l'ali del mio
amore,
e col fervido mio foco farò pago il tuo
desire.

Narcissus: *(before departing)*
I hurry away, with my heart light at the
prospect of happiness.
I shall fly from place to place on the
wings of love,
and I shall do your bidding with
passionate fervor.

Agrippina:
Quanto fa, quanto puote necessità di
stato, io stessa, io stessa!
Nulla più si trascuri; all'opra, all'opra!
Lode ha, chi per regnar inganno adopra.

L'alma mia fra le tempeste ritrovar spera il
suo porto.
Di costanza armato ho il petto, che d'un
regno al dolce aspetto le procelle più
funeste son oggetti di conforto.

Agrippina:
As much as destiny's decrees can do,
so I can do myself!
Overlook nothing! To work, to work!
Praise the one who deceives so he can reign.

Amidst the tempest, my soul hopes to
reach its port.
So well have I armed my breast with
constancy, that with fair land in sight,
even baleful storms seem to comfort.

The square in front of the Capitol.

Nerone:
Qual piacere a un cor pietoso l'apportar
sollievo ai miseri!
Prendi tu ancora, prendi!
Ma rassembra tormentoso il veder fra
turba tante che vi manchi un zelo amante
ch'il lor stato almen commiseri.

Amici, al sen vi stringo. Oh come
volentieri di voi io stesso invece la dura
povertà soffrir vorrei!
(Servon arte ed inganno a' desir miei!)

Nero: *(Distributing gifts to the populace)*
What pleasure it affords a kind heart
to bring relief to the wretched!
Here, you must have some too.
Yet it grieves me to see that amidst these
crowds you have no zealous supporter to
commiserate your state.

My friends, I embrace you;
oh, with what pleasure. I would take your
cruel suffering upon myself!
(May cunning and deceit serve my ends!)

Pallante, Narciso:
Ecco chi presto fia Cesare a Roma.

Pallas, Narcissus:
This man shall soon be Rome's emperor.

Pallante:
(Si concili il suo amor.)

Pallas:
(One must win his affection.)

Narciso:
(Merto s'acquisti.)

Narcissus:
(One must acquire his favor.)

Pallante:
Qui, Signore, risplende la tua virtù.

Pallas:
In these acts, sir, your virtue shines out.

Narciso:
La tua pietà qui spande a incatenar i cor, e
gloria e fama.

Narcissus:
Your tender mercy, displayed here, is such
as to win hearts, glory, and fame.

Nerone:
Ah Pallante, ah Narciso!
Duolmi che angusto fato sia termine a mie
brame.

Nero:
Ah Pallas, ah Narcissus!
It aches me that miserly fate constrains
my yearning.

A tutti col desir giovar vorrei; pietade è la
virtù più grata a' Dei.
(Madre i precetti tuoi non abbandono,
che, se finger saprò, Cesare sono.)

I would help all the needy: compassion is
a virtue most pleasing to the gods.
(Mother, do not abandon our principals:
if I must pretend, I shall become emperor.)

Pallante:
Agrippina qui vien.

Pallas:
Agrippina comes.

Narciso:
E accompagnata da ogn'ordine di gente;
alto affar la conduce.

Narcissus:
And accompanied by people of every
rank. Weighty matters brings her.

Pallante:
Tu forse lo saprai?

Pallas:
Perhaps you know of it?

Narciso:
Qual sia m'è ignoto.

Narcissus:
What it may be, I do not know.

Narciso, Pallante:
(Agrippina a me sol tutto fé noto)

Pallas, Narcissus:
(Agrippina made known all to me alone.)

Nerone:
(Questo è il giorno fatal del mio destino)

Nero:
(On this day my destiny will be decided.)

Narciso, Pallante:
(Presto spero goder volto divino)

Narcissus, Pallas:
(Soon I shall revel in her lovely features.)

Agrippina seats herself on the throne.

Agrippina:
Voi che dall'alta Roma coll'amor
col consiglio e colla forza i casi dirigete,
a voi qui regno apportatrice infausta
di funesta novella.

Agrippina:
You who with love, wisdom and strength
direct the fortunes of lofty Rome, to you
I come, the unhappy bearer
of dreadful tidings.

Amici è morto Claudio. L'infido mar,
geloso che restasse alla terra un tal tesoro,
lo rapì a noi.
Di Roma fatto è vedovo il soglio.

My friends. Claudius is dead; the
treacherous sea, envious of such a treasure
left on land, has snatched him from us; the
throne of Rome has created a widow.
(She descends from the throne)

L'autorità, ch'è in voi, scelga un Cesare al
trono, ed egli sia giusto, pietoso e pio
qual merta Roma e il mio cor desia.

May your authority choose another
emperor; let him be just, merciful, and pious,
as Rome deserves, and my heart desires.

Pallante:
Il tuo figlio...

Pallas:
Your son...

Narciso:
La tua prole...

Narcissus:
Your offspring...

Narciso, Pallante:
...merta sol scettro e corone;
viva, viva Nerone, viva!

Narcissus, Pallas:
...he deserves the scepter and crown;
long live Nero!

Agrippina:
Viva, viva Nerone, viva!
Vieni, oh figlio, ascendi al trono, vieni, oh
Cesare, di Roma!

Agrippina:
Long live Nero!
Come, my son, ascend the throne.
Come, emperor of Rome!

Nerone:
Nel mio cor l'alma è gioliva.
Al regnar giunto già sono, vengo a cinger
d'allor la chioma.

Nero:
My soul rejoices within me.
Now I shall reign, now I shall wreathe my
locks with laurel.

Agrippina and Nero ascend the throne.

Agrippina:
Ma qual di liete trombe odo insolito suono?

Agrippina:
But what sound of joyous trumpets do I hear?

Lesbo:
Allegrezza, allegrezza!
Claudio giunge d'Anzio al porto;
che del mar ch'il volle assorto, domò
Otton l'alta fierezza.

Lesbus:
O joy! Rejoice!
Claudius is arrived at the port of Anzio;
Otho subdued the vaunting pride of the
ocean that wished him drowned.

Pallante:
Che sento!

Pallas:
What do I hear?

Narciso:
Crudo ciel!

Narcissus:
O cruel heavens!

Agrippina:
Perfido fato!

Agrippina:
Treacherous fate!

Nerone:
Evvi al mondo di me più sfortunato?

Nero:
Is anyone in the world as wretched as I?

Agrippina:
Non ti turbino, o figlio, gl'influssi del
destin per te funesti;
quel soglio ascenderai donde scendesti.
(Se ma d'arte fu d'uopo, ora l'arte
s'adopri)
Oh qual contento, amici, nasce al mio
cuore afflitto:
Claudio è risorto, ed è risorta ancora la
fortuna di Roma.
Per novella sì lieta l'allegrezza comun
sorga festiva!

Agrippina:
My son, do not allow the slings and
arrows of outrageous fortune trouble you;
you shall ascend the throne.
(If ever cunning were needed, let it now be
employed.)
Oh what contentment, my friends, is born
within my afflicted heart:
Claudius is risen from the dead, and the
fortunes of Rome have risen with him.
At such happy news let common joy
spring forth gladly!

Coro:
Evviva Claudio, evviva!

Chorus:
Long live Claudius!

Narciso:
(Oh contenti perduti!)

Narcissus:
(Oh, my lost happiness!)

Pallante:
(Oh speranze smarrite!)

Pallas:
(My hopes are dashed!)

Nerone:
(Empi cieli, così voi mi tradite?)

Nero:
(Pitiless heaven, thus you betray me?)

Lesbo:
Signora, a te sen viene il valoroso Ottone,
che dai gorghi del mar Cesare trasse,
e lo ripone al soglio.

Lesbus:
My lady, to you come the valiant Otho,
who dragged Caesar from the ocean's jaws
and restored him to land.

Agrippina, Nerone, Narciso, Pallante:
(Vien la fiera cagion del mio cordoglio)

Agrippina, Nero, Narcissus, Pallas:
(Here is the main cause of my affliction.)

Lesbo:
(Ratto volo a Poppea nunzio d'amore,
i sensi a discoprir, che Claudio ha il
cuore.)

Lesbus:
(I shall be a messenger of love and fly
swiftly to Poppea to reveal to her the
feelings Claudius nurtures in his breast.)

Ottone:
Alle tue piante, oh Augusta,
tra le sventure fortunato io torno.
Già de' Britanni vinti mentre il mar porta
gonfio il gran trionfo, invido ancor
tra le procelle tenta a Roma di rapirlo.

Otho:
Fortunately, I return, Augusta, to kneel
before you.
As soon as Britain was defeated, the sea
surged, and envious of our triumph tried
to plunder it from Rome.

Men forti, quanto carche cedon le navi
al tempestoso nembo. Chi tra scogli
s'infrange; chi dall'onde è sommerso;
né rispetto a Regnante ha il flutto infido,
e dal plebeo indistinto a sé lo trasse, da
ogn'un creduto estinto.

Our ships gave way before the storm, and
were too weak to bear their loaded cargoes
as we were shattered by treacherous
waves and submerged between rocks.
The Emperor was dragged down into the
sea until all believed that he was dead.

Ma per amico fato nel naufragio comun il
braccio forte sovra gli omeri miei lo tolse a
morte.

But thanks to kindly fate, my strong arm
fought the wreck and brought him forth
from death.

Agrippina:
Per opra così grande Claudio, Roma,
Agrippina tutto a te denno, e da un'anima
augusta la mercede maggior sarà più
giusta.

Agrippina:
For such a great deed, Claudius, Rome and
Agrippina are all in your debt,
and from the soul of a Caesar a greater
reward shall be more fitting.

Ottone:
Già del grato Regnante sorpassa il merto
mio la ricompensa.
Di Cesare nel grado ei mi destina al soglio.

Otho:
Already a grateful monarch's reward has
surpassed my expectations; Caesar's
benevolence appoints me to the throne.

Narciso, Pallante:
(Che sento, oh ciel!)

Narcissus, Pallas:
(Oh heavens, what do I hear?)

Agrippina:
(Cesare?)

Agrippina:
(Caesar?)

Nerone:
(Ahi, che cordoglio!)

Nero:
(Alas, what anguish!)

Ottone:
Allo spuntar della novella aurora
mirerà trionfante Roma il suo Claudio,
e allora al popolo, al Senato ei farà noto
l'onor che mi comparte.

Otho:
At daybreak, Rome will marvel at her
triumphant Claudius, and he will then
make known to the people and the Senate
the honor he bestows upon me.

Agrippina:
Onor a te dovuto.

Agrippina:
An honor well deserved!

Pallante:
Otton dunque sarà...

Pallas:
Then Otho shall be...

Narciso:
Cesare fia?

Narcissus:
He shall be Caesar?

Agrippina:
(Cederò prima estinto)

Agrippina:
(Over my dead body!)

Nerone:
(Ah gelosia)

Nero:
(Alas, what jealousy I suffer!)

Ottone:
Se'l permetti, oh Signora,
occulto arcano a te svelar vorrei,
da cui solo dipende tutto ciò ch'è più lieto
ai desir miei.

Otho: *(to Agrippina)*
If you will permit me, my lady,
I would reveal to you a weighty secret,
upon which all that is most dear to my
heart depends.

Agrippina:
(Costui cauta s'ascolti)
Eh voi partite!
Confida a me, confida quanto il tuo cor
desia.

Agrippina:
(Let us listen with circumspection.)
You others may leave.
Confide in me and tell me what is your
heart's desire?

Narciso:
(Crudo ciel!)

Pallante:
(Strani eventi)

Nerone:
(Ahi sorte ria!)

Ottone:
Augusta, amo Poppea. Trono, scettro non curo;
se privo io son dell'adorato bene;
a cui soggetto il viver mio si rende,
da te la mia fortuna oggi dipende.

Agrippina:
Nutra pure il tuo core
sensi d'amore per la beltà gradita,
ch'il mio pronto sarà per darti aita.

Ottone:
Oh magnanima e grande dispensiera di grazie, e di fortune, quanto, quanto a te devo!

Agrippina:
(Ama Claudio Poppea, ciò m'è già noto;
spero ch'il mio pensier non vada a vuoto.)

Tu ben degno sei dell'allor,
(ma di sdegno arde il mio cor.)
Con l'oggetto che fa il tuo amor avrai nel petto dolce l'ardor.

Ottone:
L'ultima del gioir meta gradita tu mi porgi, oh fortuna!
Oggi al trono, per rendermi beato, unirà Amor un divin volto e amato.

Lusinghiera mia speranza, l'alma mia non ingannar!
Sorte, placida in sembianza, il bel volto non cangiar!

Narcissus:
(Cruel heavens!)

Pallas:
(What a turn of events!)

Nero:
(Alas, treacherous fate!)

Otho:
Augusta, I love Poppea: I have no interest
in the throne or scepter,
my fate depends on you;
so do not deprive me
of my life and love.

Agrippina:
Let your passion for this beauty
sustain your heart, for my heart will be
ready to assist you.

Otho:
You are a great and magnanimous.
You bestow favors and blessings.
I owe you so much!

Agrippina:
(Claudius loves Poppea; I know that;
I hope it doesn't ruin my plans.)

You are worthy of the laurel.
(But my heart is aflame with anger.)
a gentle flame burns in your breast for the
one who inspires your love.

Otho:
How fortunate that you support me on
the very summit of happiness!
To bless me, love has united the gift of the
throne with my beloved.

My flattery does not deceive what is in
my heart!
Smiling fate, do not change your
countenance!

Poppea's chamber. She stands before a mirror.

Poppea:
Vaghe perle, eletti fiori, adornatemi la
fronte!
Accrescete a mia bellezza la vaghezza,
che a svegliar nei petti amori ho nel cor le
voglie pronte.

Otton, Claudio, Nerone la lor fiamma
hanno scoperto.
D'essi ciascuno il proprio ardor lusinga;
né sanno ancor s'io dica il vero o finga.

Poppea:
Adorn my brow, precious pearls, and
choice flowers!
Increase my rare beauty,
and awaken love in men's hearts;
desire is ready in my heart.

Otho, Claudius and Nero have all revealed
their passion. Each one is flattered by his
own ardor; and no longer knows if I speak
the truth or deceive.

Lesbo:
Signora, o mia Signora!

Lesbus:
My lady, oh my lady!

Poppea:
(Questi è il servo di Claudio; non si lascin
d'amor gl'inganni e l'arte)
Oh fido servo, oh quanto mi consola il
vederti!
E quai di Claudio nuove liete m'apporti?

Poppea:
(Here is Claudius's servant: let us
maintain love's deception and cunning.)
Faithful servant, the sight of you brings
me comfort!
Do you bring me good news from Claudius?

Lesbo:
Là del mar ne' perigli più che il perder se
stesso, la tua memoria afflitto le rendea;
invocava in aiuto ciascuno i Numi suoi,
egli Poppea.

Lesbus:
During his peril, he became wretched,
more preoccupied with thoughts of his
wife rather than loss of is own life. Each
called on his gods; he called on Poppea.

Poppea:
O caro Lesbo, esprimere abbastanza non
posso il rio dolore, che al cor donò sì dura
lontananza.
Momento non passò, ch'al mio pensier ei
non fosse presente,
(Mio cor, tu sai come la lingua mente)

Poppea:
Ah, dear Lesbus, I cannot find words
to describe the awful sorrow such a painful
separation has brought to my heart.
Not a moment went by when he was not
in my thoughts.
(My heart, well you know I lie to you.)

Lesbo:
Di lieta nuova apportator io sono.

Lesbus:
Then I am the bearer of good news.

Agrippina:
(Il servo è qui, s'ascolti!)

Agrippina: *(aside)*
(Let's see what that servant has to say!)

Poppea:
E che, dimmi!

Poppea:
Pray, tell me!

Lesbo:
Solo tacito, e ascoso in questa notte
oscura verrà Claudio da te.

Lesbus:
Alone, in silence and in secret, this very
night, Claudius will come to you.

Poppea:
(Cieli, che sento!)
Ma Agrippina?

Poppea:
(Heavens, what do I hear!)
But what about Agrippina?

Lesbo:
Non dubitar, Signora; io vigile custode
sarò per ogni parte.

Lesbus:
Have no fear, my lady. I shall keep careful
watch all around here.

Poppea:
Che farò mai?

Poppea:
What shall I do?

Lesbo:
Già l'ora s'avvicina; dalla reggia non lunge
egli m'attende;
penosa a un cor, ch'adora d'un sol omento
la tardanza rende.

Lesbus:
The hour is at hand: he awaits for me in
the palace, close by.
A single moment's delay can be painful to
a loving heart.

Poppea:
Venga Claudio, ma sappia, ch'il mio cor,
se ben suo, nella sua purità sempre è
costante.
L'accolgo qual sovran, non qual amante.

Poppea:
Then let Claudius come, but he must
understand that my heart,
is ever constant in its purity:
I welcome him as sovereign, not as lover.

Lesbo:
Io tanto non vi cerco; io parto, addio!

Lesbus:
I ask no more: I leave, farewell!

Agrippina:
(Il destino seconda il desir mio!)

Agrippina:
(Fate seconds my wishes!)

Poppea:
Perché in vece di Claudio il caro Otton
non viene?
Ei più gradito sarebbe al cor, che l'ama;
ma tardo arriva ognor quel che si brama.

Poppea:
Why does dear Otho not come instead of
Claudius? He would be more welcome to
a heart that loves him; but what one longs
for is always slow in arriving.

È un foco quel d'amore che penetra nel
core, ma come? non si sa.
S'accende a poco a poco, ma poi non
trova loco e consumar ti fa.

Love is a fire that enters the heart.
But how? No one knows.
It ignites very slowly, but then grows
more intense and burns you completely.

(Ma qui Agrippina viene.
Che farò mai, se Claudio giunge?
Ahi pene!)

(But here comes Agrippina.
What shall I do if Claudius arrives.
Ah, what conflicts!)

Agrippina:
Poppea, tu sa che t'amo, e a me communi
son di pena o piacer i casi tuoi.

Agrippina:
Poppea, you know that I love you,
and I am concerned for you — good or ill.

Poppea:
(Se Claudio vien, dal ciel imploro aita.)

Poppea:
(If Claudius arrives I'll cry for heaven's help.)

Agrippina:
(Spero ch'il fine avrà la frode ardita.)
Dimmi senza rossor, Ottone adori?

Agrippina:
(I hope to see an end to this intrigue.)
Without blushing, do you love Otho?

Poppea:
Ah! non oso, Agrippina!

Poppea:
Ah, Agrippina, I dare not say!

Agrippina:
A me confida i sensi del tuo cor.

Agrippina:
Confide in me. What does your heart feel?

Poppea:
È ver, l'adoro.

Poppea:
Then it's true, I love him with a passion.

Agrippina:
Sappi ch'ei ti tradisce. Conscio che
Claudio mira con amor il tuo bello,
ei si prevalse d'un enorme delitto.
Per secondar d'ambizione oscura del cor
gl'impulsi egli a Claudio cesse, purché
Cesare in soglio oggi lieto l'adori il
Campidoglio.

Agrippina:
Then know that Otho betrays you;
Claudius looks longingly on your beauty,
he undertakes to do you a terrible wrong.
Giving way to the stirrings of secret
ambition in his heart, Claudius promised
the throne to Otho; and in return,
Claudius will receive your love.

Poppea:
E tanto è ver?

Poppea:
Can all this be true?

Agrippina:
E tanto io t'assicuro, e, del mio dir in
prova, in questa notte ancora nascoso
a te verrà Claudio fra l'ombre.

Agrippina:
I assure you, it is true. To confirm what I
say, know that this very night Claudius
will come to you, hidden by the darkness.

Poppea:
(Ciò ad Agrippina è noto?)

Poppea:
(Agrippina knows all about it!)

Agrippina:
Senti! Claudio tosto verrà:
tu accorta alla vendetta attendi.

Agrippina:
Listen: Claudius will be here soon;
prepare your revenge.

Poppea:
Che far degg'io?

Poppea:
What should I do?

Agrippina:
Ore penetri gelosia. Mesta ti fingi, di,
ch'Ottone superbo, nel nuovo grado
audace t'obbliga a non mirarlo,
e te desia; perché da sé scacci, lusinghe,
vezzi adopra, e s'egli amor pretende,
prometti amor, piangi, sospira e prega.

Nulla però concedi se prima al tuo desir ei
non si piega.

Poppea:
Tanto pronta farò; ma se acconsente,
di mie promesse il frutto vorrà goder,
ed io qui, inerme e sola, come fuggir potrò
si gran periglio!

Agrippina:
Segui senza temer il mio consiglio.

Ho un non so che nel cor, che invece di
dolor, gioia mi chiede.
Ma il cor, uso a temer le voci del piacer
o non intende ancor, o inganno del
pensier, forse le crede.

Poppea:
Cieli, quai strani casi conturbano la mente!
Ottone, Ottone!
Queste son le promesse e i giuramenti?
Così il cor ingannasti, che destinte per te
soffrir godeva le pene dell'amor?
Così tradisci per un vano splendor la fé
sincera che a me dovevi?
E audace, per soddisfar l'ambizioso ardire,
offri me in olocausto al tuo desire?

Fa quanto vuoi gli schemi tuoi non
soffrirò.
Dentro al mio petto sdegno e vendetta
risveglierò.

Lesbo:
Non veggo alcun. Signora, Claudio è qui.
Non temer, vieni sicuro; tutto è in muto
silenzio, ne men dell'aura il sussurrar qui
s'ode; a tuoi piacer Argo sarò custode.

Agrippina:
Make jealousy enter Claudius's heart; feign
sadness, say that emboldened Otho,
insists that you not see Claudius: that he
desires you. Keep Claudius away with
tricks, flattery and tricks; if he declares his
love, promise love, weep, sigh, and beg.

Concede nothing, however, until he first
bows to your wishes.

Poppea:
I am ready to do that; but if he yields, he
will want to enjoy the fruit of my promises,
and I am here all alone and undefended.
How can I ward off so great a danger?

Agrippina:
Follow my advice fearlessly.

Something in my heart, instead of sorrow
prompts joy; but I accustom my heart to
fear the voices of pleasure.
Either it no longer listens, or because of the
mind's trickery the heart believes them.

Poppea:
All heavens, what strange events disturb
my peace of mind! Otho, Otho, are these
your promises, your vows?
Do you thus deceive the heart which such
love for you?
Do you betray vain splendor for the sake
of the sincere loyalty you owed me, and
rashly, to satisfy your ambitions, offer me
in sacrifice to your wishes?

Do what you will, I shall not suffer
your mockery!
Within my soul I shall awaken scorn and
vengeance.

Lesbus:
It is safe, my lady, Claudius is here. Fear
not, you are safe: not even the sighing
breezes can be heard; and I, Argus-like,
will stand guard over your custody.

Claudio:
Pur ritorno a rimirarvi, vaghe luci, stelle
d'amor.
Né mai stanco d'adorarvi offro in voto e
l'alma e'l cor.

Ma, oh ciel, meste e confusa a me nulla
rispondi?
Qual pensier ti conturba?
Dell'amor mio già vedi le prove più
sincere.
Deh, la doglia del cor, perché nascondi?
Parla, oh cara, rispondi.

Poppea:
Del mio interno martir già che tu vuoi
ch'io scopra la cagion, sappi.
Ma, oh Dio!

I singhiozzi del cor, misti con pianto,
permettono che appena si formi accento
tra le labbra amaro!
(Così a mentir dalla vendetta imparo.)

Claudio:
Il tuo dolor non celar; ciò che dipende dal
mio poter dispor, cara, tu puoi;
chiedi pur ciò che vuoi, tutto a te dal mio
amor sarà concesso.

Poppea:
Ah! che d'amarti più non m'è permesso!

Claudio:
E chi tel vieta?

Poppea:
Oh Dio!

Claudio:
Scopri!

Poppea:
Dir nol poss'io.

Claudio:
E chi al parlar frappone difficoltà?
Dillo, mio ben!

Claudius:
Once again I behold you in wonder,
my pretty eyes, my stars of love;
I never tired of worshipping you
I offer in tribute my soul and my heart.

But, heavens, why so sad and upset,
with nothing to say to me?
What thoughts trouble you?
You have already witnessed sincere proof
of my love.
Then why hide your heart's sorrow from
me? Speak, my dear, speak!

Poppea:
If you want me to uncover the reason
for suffering within me, then know it.
But, o god,
(She pretends to weep)
These heartfelt sobs, intermingled with
weeping, scarcely allow the words to
form on lips that have known bitterness!
(Revenge has taught me to lie like this.)

Claudius:
Do not hide your grief; you may dispose
of whatever lies within my power.
Then ask what you will, since all shall be
granted to you by my love.

Poppea:
So, I am no longer allowed to love you!

Claudius:
And who forbids you?

Poppea:
O god!

Claudius:
Tell me!

Poppea:
I cannot.

Claudius:
Who has tied your tongue?
Tell me, my dear!

Poppea:
Ottone.

Poppea:
Otho.

Claudio:
Ottone?

Claudius:
Otho?

Poppea:
Ottone sì, ch'ardito tenta far violenza al mio core.

Poppea:
Yes, Otho, who, full of pride, tries to force my affections.

Claudio:
Tutto di'! Che mai sento! Oh traditore!

Claudius:
Tell me all; what do I hear! The traitor!

Poppea:
Scoperse, è già gran tempo, gli interni suoi desir, ma sempre in vano.
La costanza in amarti m'obbligò a disprezzarlo, e alfin noioso ei seppe la cagion del mio rigore.

Ora superbo e altiero vanta, ch'al nuovo giorno avrà del sagro allor il crine adorno.
Temerario commanda, minaccia aldanzoso se a te, mio ben, rivolge un sguardo solo.
Non è questa cagion d'immenso duolo?

Poppea:
A long time ago he revealed his secret desires to me, but to no avail: my constancy in loving you obliged me to reject him, until at last he learned to his annoyance the reason for my firmness.

Now proud and haughty, he boasts that tomorrow he shall have the sacred laurel.
Boldly he commands, impudently he threatens me if I glance on you. Isn't this reason enough for my great sorrow?

Claudio:
E tant'oltre s'avanza?

Claudius:
Does he dare to be so bold?

Poppea:
Oardito di regnar la speranza, e allor vedrai, fatto umile il superbo, a non osar di rimirarmi mai.

Poppea:
Deprive Caesar of reigning; then you will see the proud one sufficiently humbled, never to dare lift his gaze on me again.

Claudio:
Tutto farò. Non lagrimar, cor mio!

Claudius:
Leave it to me. Don't cry, dear heart!

Poppea:
Mel prometti?

Poppea:
Is that a promise?

Claudio:
Lo giuro.

Claudius:
I swear it!

Poppea:
Ottone dunque Cesare più non sarà?

Poppea:
Then Otho shall no longer be Caesar?

Claudio:
No, no, cara; in questa notte io voglio di
mia fe, del mio amor darti le prove.
Vieni tra questa braccia!
Fra dolci nodi avvinta più soavi piacer
l'alma destina.

Claudius:
No, no, my dear. This very night I wish to
show you proof of my faith and love.
Come, let me take you in my arms;
and join in a sweet embrace;
our love promises us yet sweeter pleasures.

Poppea:
(Al cimento già son;
dov'è Agrippina?)

Poppea: *(looking around)*
(The moment of crisis has arrived: where
is Agrippina?)

Claudio:
Porgi la bianca destra ad un che t'ama.
Più non tardar di consolar mie pene!

Claudius:
Give your hand to one who loves you!
Delay no longer in consoling my love!

Poppea:
(Il periglio s'accresce, e Agrippina non
viene!)

Poppea: *(looking around again)*
(The danger increases, and still Agrippina
does not come!)

Claudio:
Che rimiri, mio ben! Già custodite son da
lesbo il fido le regie soglie.
Vieni ad appagar, o cara, il mio desire!

Claudius:
What are you staring at, my love?
The royal thresholds are guarded by the
faithful Lesbus. Come, assuage my desire!

Poppea:
(Né pur giunge Agrippina; ahi; che
martire!)

Poppea:
(No sign of Agrippina. Ah, what
torment!)

She turns and looks around again.

Claudio:
Vieni, oh cara, ch'in lacci stretto
dolce diletto Amor prepara.

Claudius:
Come, my dear, to my tight embrace
love may prepare our sweet delight!

Poppea:
(Che mai farò?)

Poppea:
(What shall I do!)

Claudio:
T'intendo! Donna casta talor vuol per
escusa che s'usi la violenza.
Al mio voler non ripugnar, cor mio!

Claudius:
I understand! A chaste woman sometimes
wants the excuse that she is taken by
force. Do not fight me off, my beloved!

Lesbo:
Signor, Signor, presto fuggiamo!
Viene la tua sposa Agrippina.

Lesbus: *(rushing in)*
My lord, we must flee immediately!
Here comes your wife Agrippina.

Claudio:
Crudo ciel!

Claudius:
Cruel heavens!

Lesbo:
Non tardar!

Lesbus:
Do not delay!

Poppea:
(Fuggon le pene!)

Poppea:
(My, troubles are over!)

Claudio:
Lesbo, l'adito chiudi!

Claudius:
Lesbus, lock the door!

Lesbo:
Più non è tempo.

Lesbus:
There isn't time.

Poppea:
Ah, Claudio di te, si me si caglia;
parti, Signor, se m'ami!

Poppea:
Ah, Claudius, you're lost as well as I.
Leave, sir, if you love me!

Claudio:
E sarò privo del bramato piacer?

Claudius:
And be deprived of my pleasure?

Lesbo:
Non più consiglio.

Lesbus:
This is no time to argue!

Poppea:
(Giunse a tempo Agrippina al mio
periglio.)

Poppea:
(Agrippina arrives just in time to save
me.)

Claudio:
E quando mai i frutti del mio amor, bella,
godrò?

Claudius:
And when, my lovely, shall I enjoy your
love?

Poppea:
Quando vorrai!

Poppea:
Whenever you wish!

Lesbo:
Partiam, Signor!

Lesbus:
Let's go, my lord!

Claudius and Lesbus depart.

Poppea:
Pur la fin se ne andò. Lieto mio core,
oggi vedrai punito il traditore!

Poppea:
At last he has gone! Today my happy
heart will see the traitor punished.

Poppea:
O mia liberatrice, quanto a te devo,
e quanto da tuoi saggi consigli il frutto
attendo!

Poppea:
O my liberator, how much I owe you, and
how eagerly I await the results of your
good advice!

Agrippina:

Agrippina:
Nascosa il tutto intesi:
oggi sarem compagne a mirar liete più il
nostro che di Cesare il trionfo.
T'abbraccio, amica, e in me tutto confida;
disponi, oh cara, del mio cor che t'ama.
(Felice riuscì l'ordita trama)

Agrippina:
Hidden, I heard all.
Today we shall be happy companions in
love, rather than Caesar's triumph.
I embrace you, my dear. Confide
everything to me. Trust my loving heart.
(A tangled web unwinds to a happy ending.)

Poppea:
Augusta, il mio voler da te dipende.

Poppea:
Augusta, my very will depends on you.

Agrippina:
Non ho cor che per amarti, sempre amico
a te sarà.
Con sincero e puro affetto io ti stringo a
questo petto;
mai di frodi, inganni ed arti sia tra noi
l'infedeltà.

Agrippina:
My heart exists only for your love;
I shall always be your friend.
With pure and sincere affection,
I embrace you;
never fraud, deceit or infidelity shall exist
between us.

Poppea:
Se Ottone m'ingannò, e s'egli ingrato
un dolce amor al fasto suo soggetta,
del cor offeso è giusto la vendetta.

Poppea:
If Otho has deceived me, and if the ingrate
spurns the sweetness of love for pomp,
the vengeance of my betrayal is just.

Se giunge un dispetto a' danni del cor,
si cangia nel petto l'amore in furor.
Non ama chi offende o segue l'Amor,
il cor si difende, da efimero ardor.

If something damaging wounds my heart,
love changes to fury in the soul.
An offender neither loves, nor follows.
Cupid; defend us from momentary passion.

END of ACT I

Act II

A street in Rome next to the imperial palace, decorated for Claudius's triumph.

Pallante:
Dunque noi siam traditi?

Pallas:
So, we have been tricked?

Narciso:
Amico, è vero ciò ch'a te dissi.

Narcissus:
My friend, what I told you is true.

Pallante:
E quel ch'io ti narrai dubbio non ha.

Pallas:
And what I told you is not to be doubted.

Narciso:
Sia dunque la fè tra noi, qual nell'inganno
è d'uopo.

Narcissus:
Let us then keep faith with one another,
as is needed when in such subterfuge.

Pallante:
Se delude Agrippina, l'arte con lei
s'adopri.

Pallas:
If Agrippina mocks us, we must use
cunning against her.

Narciso:
Sì, sì, la frode scopra il finger nostro,
e qual ch'a te ricerca a me pronto dirai,
ed io prometto a te fido svelar quanto a
me chiede.

Narcissus:
Yes, yes, our pretense shall uncover her
deception; whatever she asks, do tell me
immediately, just as I promise to reveal to
you whatever she asks of me.

Narciso, Pallante:
A noi la destra sia pegno di fede!

Narcissus, Pallas:
Let our right hands pledge our fidelity!

Pallante:
Ottone giunge.

Pallas:
Here is Otho.

Narciso:
E questi esser Cesare deve!

Narcissus:
The one who is to be Caesar!

Pallante:
Già gli ossequi di tutti egli riceve.

Pallas:
He already receives universal homage.

Ottone:
Coronato il crin d'alloro io sarò nel
campidoglio.
Ma più bramo il bel ch'adoro, che non fò
corona e soglio.

Otho:
I shall I be on the Capitol, crowned with
the laurel wreath.
But still greater is my desire for the
beauty I adore than for crown or throne.

Pallante:
Roma, più ch'il trionfo, oggi, Signor, la tua
virtude onora.

Pallas:
Today Rome honors your virtue, more
than your triumph, sir.

Narciso:
Il tuo eccelso valor la patria adora.

Narcissus:
The country bows before your lofty valor.

Ottone:
Virtù e valor bastante aver vorrei per
veder felici al Lazio i regni, e debellar
nemici.

Otho:
I would wish to own enough virtue and
valor to see Lazio's dominions happy,
and her enemies overthrown.

Pallante:
Ma dall'alto discende, per incontrar
Augusto, Poppea con Agrippina.

Pallas:
But look, from on high Poppea descends
with Agrippina to meet with Caesar.

Ottone:
Viene chi è del mio cor Diva e Regina!

Otho:
The goddess and queen of my heart has come!

Agrippina, Poppea and Nero descend from the palace with their retinues.

Agrippina:
(Ecco il superbo!)

Agrippina:
(Here is that haughty man!)

Poppea:
(Ecco l'infido!)

Poppea:
(Here is the traitor!)

Nerone:
Miro il rival, e ne sento pien d'ira il cor.

Nero:
(My rival, and my heart fills with anger.)

Agrippina:
(Poppea, fingiamo!)

Agrippina: *(aside, to Poppea)*
(Poppea, let us be cunning!)

Poppea:
(Fingiamo!)

Poppea:
(Let us be cunning!)

Ottone:
Bellissima Poppea, pur al fine mi lice
nel tuo volto bear le luci amanti.

Otho:
Most lovely Poppea, at last I may gaze in
wonder on those beloved eyes.

Agrippina:
(Come perfido egli è!)

Agrippina: *(aside, to Poppea)*
How treacherous he is!

Poppea:
(Così egli inganna!)

Poppea:
(Thus he would deceive me!)

Narciso:
(Come il duol, ch'ho nel petto, il cor
m'affanna!)

Narcissus:
(How troubling is this sorrow within my
soul!)

Ottone:
Avrà di già Agrippina del mio destin.

Otho:
Agrippina will already have told you.
what lies in store for me.

Poppea:
Già intesi il tuo desire, e quel ch'a tuo
favor oprano i fati.

Agrippina:
Quanto chiedesti, io dissi. a Poppea
(Egli volea ch'io scusassi l'error.)

Poppea:
(Ah! traditore!)

Ottone:
Quei che svelò Agrippina, sono i sensi del
core,
e ben vedrai che il piacer del trono senza
te è un affanno.

Narciso:
Vien Claudio.

Agrippina:
(Ancor resti l'inganno.)

Coro:
Di timpani e trombe al suono giulivo
il giorno festivo per tutto rimbombe!
Roma applauda il gran regnante,
Viva Claudio trionfante!

Claudio:
Nella Britannia vinta un nuovo regno al
Lazio incatenato io porto, e scelse invano,
per frastornar l'impresa, quante tempeste
ha il mar, mostri la terra;
che toglier non potrà forza d'abisso quel,
ch'il destin di Roma ha già prefisso.

Cade il mondo soggiogato e fà base al
Roman soglio.
Mà quel regno fortunato chè soggetto al
Campidoglio!

Agrippina:
Signor, quanto il mio cuore giubila nel
mirarti! E questa braccia, che, di stringerti
prive, diedero a' sensi miei sì grave pena,
ora forman d'amor dolce catena.

Poppea:
I understand your wishes, and what the
fates have arranged in your favor.

Agrippina: *(to Otho)*
I have told her of your desires.
(He wants me to excuse his misdeeds.)

Poppea:
(Ah, the traitor!)

Otho:
Agrippina has revealed my heart's desire,
and you must understand
that without you, the pleasures of the
throne would be like penance.

Nero:
Here comes Claudius.

Agrippina:
(He is timely and allows my strategy to
remain undiscovered.)

Chorus:
To the joyous clamor of trumpets and
drums our festal day resounds all over!
Rome cheers its great ruler.
Long live triumphant Claudius!

Claudius: *(upon a triumphal chariot)*
From conquered Britain, I bring a new
realm to Rome, in fetters, and in vain,
frustrate their goals. Neither all the
storms, all the earth's monsters, or even
the powers of hell shall prevent what
Rome's destiny has ordained.

Let the subjects of the world become the
foundation of the Roman throne.
It is a fortunate victory for the Roman
Capitol!

Agrippina:
My lord, how my heart rejoices to look
upon you! And these arms, which, when
denied your embrace, brought me such
suffering, now make a sweet chain of love.

Claudio:
Amabile Agrippina, pur ti restringo al
seno, che l'alma nell'amar sempre
costante: qual consorte t'abbraccio e qual
amante.

Claudius:
Lovely, Agrippina, let me clasp you once
more to my bosom, to this most constant
and loving of hearts.
As a consort I embrace you, and as a lover.

Poppea:
Cesare, io pur l'alte tue glorie onoro.

Poppea:
Caesar, I too honor your great triumphs.

Claudio:
Aggradisco il tuo dir.

(Sa che t'adoro!)

Claudius:
I am grateful for your words.
(aside, to Poppea)
(You know how I adore you!)

Nerone:
Della mia fè divota offro i tributi.

Nero
I offer tribute for my faithful devotion.

Claudio:
Figlio, sei certo del mio amor.

Claudius:
My son, be sure of my love.

Narciso:
Ossequioso venero le tue glorie.

Narcissus:
I worship your glory with deep humility.

Pallante:
E de' trionfi spande Fama immortal per
tutto il suono.

Pallas:
And the immortal fame of your triumphs
spread far and wide.

Claudio:
Di Narciso e Pallante gli affettuosi pensier
noti mi sono.

Claudius:
I am aware of the tender thoughts of
Narcissus and Pallas.

Ottone:
Alle tue piante, Augusto, ecco prostrato
Ottone, il tuo fedel, che là nel mar.

Otho:
Great Caesar, behold your faithful Otho
lying at your feet, arriving from the sea.

Claudio:
Che vuoi?

Claudius:
What do you want?

Ottone:
Alla mia fede, Signor, attendo umile
la promessa mercede.

Otho:
In faith, my lord, I humbly await my
promised reward.

Claudio:
E hai l'ardir di comparirmi innante?

Claudius:
You have the temerity to appear before me?

Ottone:
Di quel fallo son reo?

Otho:
Of what fault am I guilty?

Claudio:
Sei traditore!

Nerone, Narciso, Pallante:
(Che sento mai?)

Agrippina:
(Va ben!)

Poppea:
(Giubila, o core!)

Ottone:
Io traditor? Io, che fra rischi ardito,
senza temer la morte, dalla morte ti trassi,
io traditore?

Claudio:
Non più, ch'al tuo fallir giusta pena è il
morir.

Ottone:
Cieli, ch'intendo!

Claudio:
(Ma a chi vita mi diè la vita io rendo.)

Ottone:
Deh tu, Agrippina, assisti!

Agrippina:
Nulle sperar da me, anima senza fè,
cor traditore!
Fasto che t'abbagliò, perché non t'additò
cotanto orrore?

Ottone:
Soccorri almen Nerone!

Poppea:
Tuo ben è 'l trono, io non son più tuo
ben. È quello il tuo contento,
ed io per te ne sento la gioia del mio sen.

Ottone:
Scherzo son del destin. Narciso, amico,
compatisci quel duol ch'il seno aduna?

Claudius:
You are a traitor!

Nero, Narcissus, Pallas:
(What is this I hear?)

Agrippina:
(Very well!)

Poppea:
(Rejoice, o my heart!)

Otho:
I a traitor? Who braved mortal dangers
fearlessly to pluck you from death?
I am a traitor?

Claudius:
Enough! For your transgression,
death is the proper reward.

Otho:
Heavens, what do I hear!

Claudius:
(For the one who saved my life, pardon.)

Otho:
Agrippina, come to my aid!

Agrippina:
Expect no help from me, you faithless,
treacherous man!
Your vicious crime was dazzled by
splendor, and not apparent to you?

Otho:
And you, Poppea, my beloved?

Poppea:
Your beloved is the throne, no longer me.
Of the laurels of the throne lies your
happiness, and I am very happy for you!

Otho:
Help me, my friend Narcissus, and pity
the sadness in my soul?

Narciso:
L'amico dura sol quanto fortuna.

Narcissus:
A friend remains true only as long as fortune.

Ottone:
Habbi pietà tu almeno di quest'alma
penante?

Otho:
Will you at least take pity on my
tormented soul!

Pallante:
Chi ad Augusto è nemico, è nemico a
Pallante.

Pallas:
He who is Caesar's enemy, is also an
enemy of Pallas.

Ottone:
Lesbo fedel, compiangi al mio dolore!

Otho:
Faithful Lesbus, weep and share my grief!

Lesbo:
Lesbo sdegna ascoltar un traditore.

Lesbus:
Lesbus scorns giving ear to a traitor.

Ottone:
Otto, Otton, qual portentose fulmine è
questi?
Ah, ingrato Cesare, infidi amici, e Cieli
ingiusti!
Ma più del Ciel, di Claudio, o degli amici
ingiusta, ingrata ed infedel Poppea!
Io traditor? Io mostro d'infedeltà?
Ahi Cielo, ahi fato rio!
Evvi duolo maggior del duolo mio?

Otho:
Otho, what dreadful thunderbolt has
struck me!
Ah, ungrateful Caesar, faithless friends,
unjust heaven!
But how much more unjust, ungrateful
and unfaithful than heaven is Poppea!
I, a traitor? I, a monster of unfaithfulness?
Ah, heavens, ah, wicked fate!
Could any suffering be worse than mine?

Voi che udite il mio lamento, compatite il
mio dolor!
Perdo un trono, e pur lo sprezzo; ma quel
ben che tanto apprezzo, ahi che perdolo è
tormento che disanima il mio cor.

You who hear my complaint, share my
grief with me.
I lose a throne, which I despise, but my
beloved, whom I prize so greatly, what
torment for my heart to lose her.

A garden with fountains.

Poppea:
Bella pur nel mio diletto mi sarebbe
l'innocenza.
Un desio mi sento in petto che vorrebbe
usar clemenza.

Poppea:
How lovely it would be to find my
beloved innocent.
I feel an urge within me to show him
mercy.

Il tormento d'Ottone in me si fa tormento;
io pur vorrei sentir le sue discolpe.
Ma pensieroso e mesto ei qui sen viene,
forse a sfogar del cor le acerbe pene.

Otho's fate also torments me; I should
like to hear his explanation. But here he
comes, sad and thoughtful, perhaps to
unburden his heart's bitter pain.

(Par che amor sia cagion del suo martire; per scoprir meglio il vero fingerò di dormire.)

(It seems that love is the cause of his suffering; the better to uncover the truth, I'll pretend to be asleep.)

Unseen by Otho, she seats herself by a fountain, pretending to be asleep.

Ottone:
Vaghe fonti che mormorando serpeggiate nel seno all'erbe.

Otho:
Pretty streams that murmur while the wind blows along your grassy way.

Ma qui che veggo, oh ciel?
Poppea fra i fior riposa, mentre al mio fiero duol non trovo posa. Voi dormite, oh luci care, e la pace gode il core.

But what do I see, o heaven?
Poppea takes her rest amid the flowers, while I find no respite from my dreadful suffering.

Anch'il sonno, oh Dio, t'inganna, perch'io sembri un infedele!

Even sleep, o god! deceives you, since you think me unfaithful!

Poppea:
Ottone traditore!
Ingannator crudele!

Poppea: *(pretending to talk in her sleep)*
Otho betrayed me!
Cruel deceiver!

Ottone:
Dimmi almen, qual sia il fallire che cagione il tuo rigore?
(Ella si sveglia; udiamla!)

Otho:
Tell me, at least, what fault of mine engenders your coldness?
(She wakes; let me hear what she says!)

Poppea:
Fantasmi della mente, voi ancora perturbate il mio riposo?
Voi supplice al mio aspetto l'indegno traditor mi presentate?

Poppea:
Now wide awake, she appears to talk to herself. O illusions, still you disturb my peace? You present to me as suppliant the image of that unworthy traitor?

Che dirà in sua discolpa?
Negar forse potrà che a Claudio ei cesse tutto l'amor tutta la fè promessa, purché Cesare al soglio oggi Roma il vedesse in Campidoglio?

What could he say in his own defense?
Could he perchance deny that he had ceded his love and all his promised faith to Claudius, so that Rome might see him as a Caesar on the throne this day?

Ottone:
(Cieli, che sento mai?)

Otho:
(Heavens, what is this I hear?)

Poppea:
Dì pure, dimmi infido, se tradirai?
Testimonio sarà del tuo fallire Agrippina Regnante; ch'un reggio cor mentire non avrà la tua colpa ardir bastante.

Poppea:
Tell me, unfaithful one, if you will betray me?
Imperial Agrippina shall bear witness to your transgression, for your wickedness could not be so brazen as to deny royalty.

Ottone:
(Più soffrir non poss'io.)
Ecco ai tuoi piedi…
Fuggi? T'arresta, oh cara!
(Ahi che cordoglio!)
Sentimi almen!

Otho:
(I can bear no more.)
Behold at your feet …
You run from me? Stay, my dearest!
(Ah, what anguish!)
At least listen to me!

Poppea:
Sentir più non ti voglio.

Poppea:
I will listen to you no more.

Ottone:
Ferma!

Otho:
Stop!

Poppea:
Lasciami!

Poppea:
Leave me alone!

Ottone:
Senti! Prendi l'acciar, ch'alla tua destra io
dono, e se reo mi ritrovo, che tu m'uccida.
Poi contento io sono.

Otho:
Listen! Take this dagger I place in your
right hand, and if you find me guilty,
then kill me, and I will be content.

Poppea:
Parla dunque; ma avverti, che del fallo
prescritta hai già la pena.
Se traditor tu sei, cadrai vittima e sangue
in sù l'arena.

Poppea: *(she points it towards Otho)*
Speak, but be warned that the punishment
for your crime is already ordained.
If you have betrayed me, you shall
become a mortal victim right here.

Ottone:
Già intesi, non veduto, l'enormissima
accusa, che ti provoca a sdegno.
Ch'io ti ceda ad altrui?
E per un raggio di cieca ambizione te, mio
bel sole io perda?
Chi può crederlo mai, chi lo pretende?
Scettro, alloro non curo: ver te fù sempre
questo cor rivolto, che val per mille mondi
il tuo bel volto.

Otho:
Unknown, yet understood: an appalling
accusation provoking you to anger.
That I would give you up to another?
That I would let you go, my very sun,
for a single ray of blind ambition?
Who could ever believe this, who maintain
it? I care not for scepter and laurel: my
heart has always been yours, your lovely
face worth a thousand worlds.

Poppea:
Non so se creder deggia alle tue voci.
Quanto io so da Agrippina svelato fù.

Poppea:
I don't know whether to believe you.
Agrippina revealed all to me.

Ottone:
Che sento? Perfida, iniqua donna, cagion
del mio languir!
Senti, oh Poppea, quanto sia di colei
l'anima rea.

Otho:
What do I hear? That treacherous,
wicked woman, the cause of my suffering!
Hear me, o Poppea, she possesses a black
heart.

Poppea:
Ottone, or non è tempo, né cauto il luogo;
alle mie stanze vieni; il rigore sospendo.
Se tu sei reo, ver te sarò inclemente;
e pietosa m'avrai, se tu innocente.

Ottone:
Ti vò giusta e non pietosa, bella mia, nel
giudicarmi.
Tutto son, tutto innocente!
Se poi trovi il cor che mente, ti perdono il
condannarmi.

Poppea:
Di quali ordite trame ingannata son io?
Già, già comprendo le tue frodi,
Agrippina!
Per togliere ad Ottone di Cesare l'allor,
me deludesti. Ver Nerone è scoperto il
superbo pensier, che ti lusinga. Nel duol
non m'abbandono; se vendetta non fò,
Poppea non sono.

Ingannata una sol volta esser posso,
mà non più,
Quando crede il cor ascolta; mà scperta
poi la frode fassi sordo, è più non ode chi
mendace un giorno fù.

Lesbo:
Pur alfin ti ritrovo. Impaziente
Claudio di rivederti a te m'invia,
e alle tue stanze solo favellarti desia.

Poppea:
Che risolvi, oh pensier?

Lesbo:
Bella, fà core!
Che quanto ardito più, più piace amore.

Poppea:
(Bel campo alla vendetta m'offre il
destin.) Accetto il Cesareo favor.

Lesbo:
Ei verrà dunque?

Poppea:
Otho, not this time; the place is not
secure. Come to my apartments. If you
are guilty, I shall he merciless: but if
innocent, you will find me compassionate.

Otho:
I would have you just, not merciful,
my darling, in judging me.
I am completely innocent:
if then you find my heart has lied,
I shall forgive your condemnation.

Poppea:
Have I become the victim of a tangled
skein of lies?
Now, at last, I perceive her deceit!
She deceived me to snatch from Otho
Caesar's laurels. Nero, the overweening
scheme that tempted you, has been
uncovered. I shall not give way to grief.
If I don't have revenge, I am not Poppea!

I can be deceived just once, but not more.
When the heart trusts, it listens;
but once deception is uncovered it makes
itself deaf, and no longer hearkens to the
one who lied the day before.

Lesbus:
At last I find you! Impatient Claudius
wants to see you again; he sent me to
arrange a private meeting with you.

Poppea:
How shall I decide what to do?

Lesbus:
Beautiful lady, be bold, for the more
ardent the love, the more pleasure it gives.

Poppea:
(Destiny offers me a fine opportunity for
revenge.) I accept Caesar's favor.

Lesbus:
Then he may come?

Poppea:
Sì, venga pur.

Poppea:
Yes, let him come.

Lesbo:
Ad arrecar io volo nuova così grata al mio
Signore.

Lesbus:
I rush to bring such welcome news for my
lord.

Poppea:
(Cieli, voi assistete al mio disegno!)

Poppea:
(Heaven assist me in my plan!)

Lesbo:
(Oggi spero al mio oprar premio
condegno.)

Lesbus:
Today I hope for a worthy reimbursement
for my labors.)

Poppea:
A non pochi perigli mi rendo, è ver,
soggetta:
ma chi non sa temer fà la vendetta.
Il desio d'eseguirla alto pensier alla mente
m'addita. Or qui vorrei Neron.

Poppea:
I put myself in no small danger, it's true;
but he who knows no fear has his revenge.
The desire to pursue it inspires me to a
daring plan.
Now I would wish Nero was here.

Nerone:
Son qui, mia vita.

Nero:
I am here, my darling.

Poppea:
(Oh come amica sorte seconda il voti
miei!)
Senti Neron! Già mille e mille volte del
tuo amor, di tua fè giurasti il vanto.
Dubbia del vero fui, ch'à per costume
l'uom la donna ingannar, e si fa pregio
le fralezza schernir con il dispregio.

Poppea:
(Oh how propitious fate seconds my
desires!) Listen, Nero! You have sworn
your love and faith thousands of times.
I was doubtful of your sincerity,
since men are accustomed to deceive
women, and praise our frailty only to
treat it later with disdain.

Nerone:
Non temer, oh mia cara!

Nero:
Have no fear, my dearest!

Poppea:
Per ricever da te prove bastanti
malcauto è il luogo;
solo alle mie stanze vieni;
ivi, se puoi persuader il mio core,
in premi dell'amor, attendi amore!

Poppea:
To receive sufficient evidence from you
about this place is not enough.
Come alone to my apartments;
there, if you can persuade my heart,
as love's reward, you may expect love.

Nerone:
Oh mia adorata!

Nero:
Oh, my adored one!

Poppea:
Taci! Le mie offerte esseguisci e le
nascondi! Fatto l'amor palese,
in vece di piacer produce affanno.
(Spero felice il meditato inganno.)

Col peso del tuo amor misura il tuo piacer
e la tua speme!
S'è fedele il tuo cor, spera pur di goder,
e speri bene.

Nerone:
Qual bramato piacer mi s'offre del
destino!
Oggi spero baciar volto divino.

Quando invita la donna l'amante è vicino
d'amore il piacer.
Il dir: "vieni ad un istante", egli è un dir:
"vieni a goder"!

Poppea:
Hush! Do what I say, but be discreet:
love made public brings cares instead of
pleasure.
(I hope my little scheme succeeds.)

Against the weight of your love
measure your pleasure and your hope.
If you heart is faithful, it hopes for
pleasure, and your hope is well founded.

Nero:
Fate offers me a pleasure I have longed
for!
Today I hope to kiss that lovely face!

When a woman invites her lover, love's
pleasure is close at hand.
When she says: "Come immediately"
it says: "Come and enjoy yourself!"

Agrippina's apartments.

Agrippina:
Pensieri, voi mi tormentate.
Ciel, soccorri ai miei disegni!
Il mio figlio fa che regni, e voi Numi il
secondate!

Quel ch'oprai è soggetto a gran periglio.
Creduto Claudio estinto, a Narciso,
e a Pallante fidai troppo me stessa.
Ottone ha merto, ed ha Poppea coraggio,
s'è scoperto l'inganno, di riparar
l'oltraggio.
Ma fra tanti nemici a voi, frodi, or è
tempo; deh, non m'abbandonate!

Pensieri, voi mi tormentate!

Agrippina:
How you torment me, my restless mind!
May heaven aid my plans!
Let my son reign, smile upon him,
o gods!

The scheme I labor for lies in great peril.
Believing Claudius dead, I confided too
much in Narcissus and Pallas.
If my stratagem is uncovered, Otho has
the mettle and Poppea the courage
to undo the damage.
Surrounded by so many enemies, now is
the moment; ah, do not abandon me!

How you torment me, my restless mind!

Pallante:
Se ben nemica sorte non arrise a miei voti,
il cor però del tuo fedel Pallante nell'opre
sue si fè veder costante.

Pallas:
Though my unfriendly fate smiles not
upon my vows, yet your faithful Pallas's
heart ever be constant and at your service.

Agrippina:
Costante egli saria, se per me ancora
impiegarsi volesse.

Agrippina:
Then let it be constant in continuing to
serve me willingly.

Pallante:
E in che può mai a tuoi cenni ubbidir?
Bella, commanda!

Pallas:
And in what manner can I obey your
orders? Command me, my lovely one!

Agrippina:
Senti! Son miei nemici Narciso e Otton;
bramo che entrambi al suolo cadano
estinti.
Vedi, a qual rischio t'espongo!

Agrippina:
Then listen: Narcissus and Otho are my
enemies. I wish to see both of them dead.
You understand what risk I am exposing
you to.

Pallante:
Nel servirti, Agrippina, rischio non v'è
che non diventi gloria.
Ma che fia del mio amor?

Pallas:
In serving you, Agrippina, there is no risk
that is not transformed into glory.
But what will become of my love?

Agrippina:
Pallante, spera!

Agrippina:
You must hope, PalIas!

Pallante:
(Ha nel seno costei cor di Megera.)

Pallas:
(This woman has the heart of Megaera!)

Col raggio placido della speranza
la mia costanza lusinghi in me.
Così quest'anima di più non chiede
ch'è la sua fede la sua mercè.

With a mild ray of hope my constancy
leads me on.
So my heart seeks no more than her faith
and compassion.

Agrippina:
Di giunger non dispero al mio desire.
Ma qui Narciso? Ardire!

Agrippina: *(Narcissus appears)*
My will does not despair of reaching its
goal. But is this Narcissus? Let's be bold!

Or è tempo, oh Narciso, di poner fine
all'opra.
Pallante e Ottone uniti sono i nostri
nemici.
Se amor nutri per me, s'è in te coraggio,
stabilita sarà la nostra sorte.

Now is the time, Narcissus, to bring
matters to a conclusion.
United, Pallas and Otho are our joint
enemies.
If you feel love for me, and if you are
courageous, our future is secure.

Narciso:
Che debbo far?

Narcissus:
What must I do?

Agrippina:
Ad ambidue dar morte.

Agrippina:
Kill them both.

Narciso:
Tutto farò; ma infine? Qual premio avrò?

Narcissus:
I shall do all, but what shall be my final
reward?

Agrippina:
Confida, e tutto spera!

Narciso:
(Nutre costei nel sen alma di fiera!)

Spererò, poiché mel dice quel bel labbro,
oh donna Augusta!
E se spero esser felice, la mia speme, ella è
ben giusta.

Agrippina:
Per dar la pace al core, semino guerre ed
odii.
Con Claudio è 'l fin dell'opra.
Egli qui vien; mio cor, gl'inganni adopra!

Claudio:
Vagheggiar de tuoi bei lumi vengo, o cara,
il sol di viso.

Agrippina:
Vorrei della bellezza aver superba il vanto,
per goder il tuo amor; ma dove manca,
supplisce il cor, che per te sol respira.
Ma, oh Dio, nel sen s'aggira
un interno dolor, che mi tormenta,
e rende nel timor l'alma scontenta.

Claudio:
Qual t'assale timor? Scoprilo, oh cara!

Agrippina:
Preveggo in gran periglio del viver tuo la
sicurezza, e parmi d'ogni intorno sentir
strepito d'armi.

Claudio:
E chi può ardito in Roma macchiar
tradimenti?

Agrippina:
Ah mio diletto, freme ottone di sdegno;
ad ognun fia palese il grave torto.
Se pronto ad ammorzar picciola fiamma
non accorri veloce
nascerà grand'incendio alle rovine.

Agrippina:
Trust me, and you may hope for everything!

Narcissus:
(What a hard heart this woman has!)

Then I shall hope, since these lovely lips
tell me to, o regal one.
And if I hope to be happy, such hope is
reasonable.

Agrippina:
To bring peace to my heart I sow the
seeds of war and hatred.
In Claudius lies the end of my labors.
Here he comes. Prepare to deceive him!

Claudius:
I come to gaze, my sweet, on these rays
of love from your beautiful eyes.

Agrippina:
I would that I had the mighty advantage
of beauty to recompense your love;
where it lacks, my heart beats for you alone.
But, o god, an inner pain stirs within my
soul, tormenting me, and disturbing my
soul.

Claudius:
What fear assails you? Reveal it, my dear!

Agrippina:
I sense the very security of your being in
peril, and seem to hear the clash of
weapons on every side.

Claudius:
And what bold upstart could plot
betrayal in Rome?

Agrippina:
Ah, my dear one, Otho rages with
indignation, and makes known to all the
grave wrong done to him.
If one does not stifle a small flame, a
mighty, ruinous blaze will be born.

Claudio:
Che mi consigli?

Claudius:
What is your counsel?

Agrippina:
È d'uopo sveller dal suol radice velenosa.
Sin che Ottone ha speranza di salir sopra
il soglio,
il core altiero macchine tenterà, frodi ed
inganni,
troverà parziali mossi dall'interesse.

Agrippina:
It is needful to pluck a poisonous root
out of the ground.
Since Otho still hopes for the throne,
his arrogant heart will hatch schemes, lies
and stratagems; he will seek supporters
motivated by selfishness.

E la vil plebe offuscata dall'oro,
vorrà ch'ei cinga il crin del sagro alloro.
Il disdegno confondi, l'artificio previeni,
nuovo Cesare acclama immantinente!
Abbandonato ei fia, che s'adora
da ognuno il sol nascente.

Dazzled by gold, he will wish to see his
brow crowned with the sacred laurel.
Confound his schemes, forestall his
subterfuges, acclaim a new Caesar;
at a stroke Otho shall be abandoned.
for all will worship the rising sun.

Claudio:
Ma chi porrò sul trono, senza temer
che, di regnare amante,
ingrato al beneficio egli non sia?
L'autorità compagna ha gelosia!

Claudius:
But whom could I place on the throne
without fearing that, in love with power,
he would be ungrateful for my kindness?
Jealousy is the companion of authority!

Agrippina:
Credi, oh Claudio, ch'io t'ami?

Agrippina:
Do you believe, Claudius, that I love you?

Claudio:
Son certo del tuo cor.

Claudius:
Of your love I am certain.

Agrippina:
Dunque concedi per Cesare di Roma il
mio figlio Nerone!
Egli ubbidiente sarà sempre a' tuoi cenni;
il rispetto ver me, che gli son madre,
l'ossequio al cor darà ver te qual padre.

Agrippina:
Then grant my son Nero be made
Emperor of Rome!
He will be ever obedient to your wishes.
His respect for me, his mother, will make
his heart submissive to you, as a father.

Claudio:
Approvo il tuo pensier; pensiero accorto.

Claudius:
I commend your proposal, a wise notion.

Agrippina:
(Coraggio, oh cor! Siamo vicini al porto.)
Non ammetter dimora.

Agrippina:
(Courage, my heart! Our goal is close.)
Then do not delay.

Claudio:
Lascia ch'io ben rifletta all'importante
affar.

Claudius:
Let me think awhile on this important
matter.

Agrippina:
Grave periglio!

Agrippina:
The danger is acute!

Claudio:
Tutto farò, ma lascia...

Claudius:
I will do all, but leave me to...

Agrippina:
Ah non è tempo d'un indugio maggior.

Agrippina:
Ah, he who hesitates is lost.

Lesbo:
(Signor, Poppea...)

Lesbus: *(aside, to Claudius)*
(My lord, Poppea...)

Claudio:
(Parlasti?)

Claudius: *(aside, to Lesbus)*
What did you say?

Lesbo:
(Ella t'attende.)

Lesbus: *(aside, to Claudius)*
She awaits you.

Agrippina:
Periglioso si rende il perder un momento.

Agrippina:
A moment's delay puts you in peril.

Claudio:
Non dubitar, sarà il tuo cor contento.

Claudius:
Doubt not, you shall have your wish.

Agrippina:
Ma quando?

Agrippina:
But when?

Lesbo:
(Vien tosto, Signor!)

Lesbus: *(aside, to Claudius)*
(Come quickly, my lord!)

Claudio:
(Vengo)

Sarà ben tosto. Addio!
Altro affare mi porta in altro loco.

Claudius: *(aside, to Lesbus)*
(I'm coming!)
(to Agrippina)
It shall be soon. Farewell!
Another matter calls me away.

Agrippina:
No, no, non partirai, se a me tu prima ciò
non prometti.

Agrippina:
No, no, you shall not go, unless you first
promise me this.

Lesbo:
(Il tempo passa.)

Lesbus: *(aside, to Claudius)*
(Time presses.)

Claudio:
(Vengo!)

Sì, sì, sarà; prometto.

Claudius: *(aside, to Lesbus)*
(I'm coming!)
(to Agrippina)
Very well, so be it: I promise.

Agrippina:
In questo giorno Cesare fia neron, assiso in soglio?

Agrippina:
This very day, Nero shall be emperor, seated on the throne?

Claudio:
In questo dì sarà.

Claudius:
This very day.

Agrippina:
(Altro non voglio.)

Agrippina:
(I ask no more.)

Favorevol la sorte oggi m'arride.
Purché Cesare sia l'amato figlio, s'incontri ogni periglio.

Favorable fate has today smiled upon me.
As long as my beloved son is Caesar, I can meet any danger.

Ogni vento ch'al porto lo spinga,
benché fiero minacci tempeste,
l'ampie vele gli spande il nocchier.
Regni il figlio, mia sola lusinga, sian le
stelle in aspetto funeste, senza pena le
guarda il pensier.

Whatever wind blows him to port, no
matter how fierce the threatening tempest,
the mariner spreads his sails wide.
My son reigns, my one hope,
let the stars show dismal aspects,
yet those thoughts do not concern me.

END of ACT II

Act III:

Poppea's apartments.

Poppea:
Il caro Otton al precipizio io spinsi.
Ma inganno meditato, la vendetta nel cor
oggi rinchiuse, per deluder colei che mi
deluse.

Poppea:
I pushed dear Otho to the very brink,
but premeditated trickery, planted within
me a desire to avenge myself by
outwitting her, who outwitted me.

Ottone:
Ah, mia Poppea; ti prego non mi sia di
delitto un fiero tradimento; donna rea
m'ingannò, quando a mie preci del mio
amor, di mia fede esser promise
protettrice pietosa.
Del mio amor son seguace, altro non curo,
e a te, mio ben, eterna fede io giuro.

Otho:
Ah my Poppea! I pray you do not think
me guilty of this vile betrayal.
That wicked woman tricked me, when, at
my pleas, she offered sympathetic
protection to my faithful love.
I am love's follower, heeding nothing else,
and to you, beloved, I swear eternal faith.

Poppea:
Ed io con quanto ho mai di core in petto,
anima mia, l'accetto.
Per far nostra vendetta la macchina
disposi, e s'io del male fui la cagion
a me di ripararlo conviene ancora.

Poppea:
And I, with whatever heart I have within
me, my dearest, accept it.
I have made ready the means of our
revenge, and if I was the cause of harm, it
is for me to repair it.

Or qui t'ascondi e taci. Non temer di mia
fede; di ciò ch'io dica o faccia non ti
render geloso; soffrir devi per poco un rio
tormento, che in altrui sarà pene e in te
contento.

Now hide yourself here, and stay silent.
Doubt not my faith, nor be jealous
of what I may say or do. You must suffer
grievous torment, which shall result in
another's punishment, and your content.

Otho hides behind a curtain.

Poppea:
Attendo qui Nerone, e Claudio ancora;
quest'alma impaziente già s'è resa
di vendicar l'offesa.

Poppea:
I still await Nero and Claudius.
My spirit has become impatient to avenge
the offence.

Nerone:
Anelante ti reco, oh mia diletta,
a ricever mercé d'alta mia fede.

Nero:
I arrive breathless, my darling, to receive
the reward of my true faithfulness.

Poppea:
Veggo ben, ch'il tuo ardor nella tardanza
stimoli a te non diede; qual ch'a te destinai
tempo felice, trascorse già; del cor con
pena è d'uopo differirne l'effetto. Mà, oh
Dio, temo...

Poppea:
I see full well in your delay that ardor has
not spurred you on. That happy time of
your appointment is already past; it is
necessary to delay heart's cure.
But, o god. I fear...

Nerone:
Di che?

Nero:
Of what?

Poppea:
Che qui Agrippina porti il piede, e ci
scopra.

Poppea:
That Agrippina may come here, and
discover us.
(She looks around)

Nerone:
Qui dee venir la madre?

Nero:
My mother may come here?

Poppea:
E in brev'ora!
Mà acciò che tu comprenda i sensi del mio
cor, vedi qual prova io te ne dono:
quivi vuò che t'asconda, e attendi fin
ch'ella parta, e allora sciolta d'ogni timor,
vedrai quanto Poppea t'ama e t'adora.

Poppea:
And very soon!
But so that you may discern my feelings,
and see what proof I give you:
Hide yourself here, and wait till she
leaves. Then you will see how much
Poppea loves and adores you.

Nerone:
Qual già dolce piacer nel seno io sento!

Nero:
The pleasure in my soul is already sweet!

Ottone;
(Sempre più in me s'accresce il rio tormento.)

Otho:
(My cruel torment increases more.)

Nero hides in a curtain-draped doorway opposite to the one in which Otho is hidden.

Poppea:
Amico ciel, seconda il mio disegno!
Credo ch'Ottone il core avrà pieno di
sdegno; ma soffrir sempre dee chi ha in
petto amore.

Poppea:
Kindly heaven, second my plan.
I'm sure that Otho's heart is bursting with
anger: but he who loves must always
suffer.

Chi ben ama e sol brama di goder, ama
solo il suo piacer!
Quella face, cui non piace mai dolor,
non è mai d'un vero amor.

One who loves well and lusts for
pleasure, loves only his pleasure!
That face, which never likes pain,
does not express true love.

Lesbo:
Qui non v'è alcun, Signore; la piaga ch'hai
nel cor, sana d'amore.

Lesbus: *(before departing)*
There is no one here, my lord; love will
heal the wound in your heart.

Poppea:
Claudio, tu mi lusinghi, però da ver non
m'ami.

Poppea:
Claudius, you flatter me, but you do not
really love me.

Claudio:
Come? Dubbiosa ancora vivi dell'amor
mio? Cara vedesti quel ch'io feci per te!

Claudius: *(suddenly appearing)*
What? Can you still doubt my love?
My dear, you saw what I did for you!

Poppea:
Di', che facesti? Ogn'or più ardito e
audace io provo il turbator della mia pace.

Poppea:
Tell me what you did. More brazen and
daring is one who disturbs my peace.

Claudio:
Forse ancor insolente nol ritiene il castigo?

Claudius:
Perhaps the impudent man does not
consider the punishment adequate?

Poppea:
E qual castigo?

Poppea:
What punishment is that?

Claudio:
Ei, balzato dal soglio, nutre ancora tanto
orgoglio?

Claudius:
Can one thrown off the throne still harbor
such audacity?

Poppea:
Non t'intendo, Signor, e più che mai di
salirvi ha speranza.

Poppea:
I do not understand, my lord; he more
than ever hopes to ascend the throne.

Claudio:
E risiede in Otton tanta baldanza?

Claudius:
Could Otho harbor such effrontery?

Poppea:
D'Otton? Signor, che parli? Ah Claudio,
già comprendo la mia sorte fatal, la mia
sventura.

Poppea:
Otho? What do say? Ah, Claudius, at last
I understand my fatal ill-luck and my
misfortune.
(She pretends to weep)

Claudio:
Bella, tu piangi? Dimmi che deggio far?
Imponi!
Come già ti promisi, dalle tempia 'Ottone
tolsi l'alloro.

Claudius:
You weep, my lovely? Tell me, what must
I do!
Order me! As I promised you before, the
laurel shall he plucked from Otho's brow.

Nerone:
(Che pena è non udir!)

Nero:
(If only I could hear what they are saying!)

Ottone:
(Soffro e non moro?)

Otho:
(I suffer this, and do not die?)

Poppea:
Dalle tempia d'Ottone?

Poppea:
From Otho's brow?

Claudio:
D'Ottone sì, ch'ardito leggi al tuo cor
impone.

Claudius:
Yes, that bold man who lays down
laws for your love.

Poppea:
Otton, Signor, non fù.

Claudio:
Ma chi?

Poppea:
Nerone! Per Nerone esclamai, ei mi vietò
di non mirarti mai.

Claudio:
Come? Ottone dicesti.

Poppea:
Neron dissi, Signor, mal intendesti.

Claudio:
Neron? Come s'accorda il desio di regnar,
lo scettro, il soglio? Tu m'inganni, oh
Poppea!

Poppea:
Io t'inganno? Signor, forse non sai ch'il
desio d'Agrippina, pria che giungesti in
Roma, sieder lo fè sul trono, ed acclamato
Cesare fù; meco tu fingi ancora?

Nerone:
(E ancor non parte, oh ciel!)

Ottone:
(Il duol m'accora!)

Claudio:
Che mi narri di strano!
Ma non dicesti Otton?
Dimmi, rispondi!

Poppea:
Signore, forse prendesti con equivoco il
nome; han Nerone ed Ottone un egual
suono.

Claudio:
Quel ch'io creda non sò, stupido io sono.

Poppea:
That wasn't, my lord, Otho.

Claudius:
But who then?

Poppea:
It was Nero! I complained, and he
forbade me to gaze on you ever again.

Claudius:
What? You said Otho!

Poppea:
Nero, my lord. You did not understand.

Claudius:
Nero? And all that talk of Otho's desire to
reign, to wield the scepter and sit on the
throne? You have deceived me, Poppea!

Poppea:
I deceived you? You did not know that
before you reached Rome, at Agrippina's
wish, Nero was raised to the throne, and
acclaimed Caesar? Are you just pretending?

Nero:
(Oh heavens, if only he would leave!)

Otho:
(The pain is killing me!)

Claudius:
What strange things you tell me!
But didn't Otho tell you?
Come, answer me!

Poppea:
My lord, perhaps you mixed the two
names up. Nero and Otho sound much
alike.

Claudius:
I don't know; how confusing this is.

Poppea:
Dubiti ancor? D'ogn'uno del mio dir farò
fede, e, se tu vuoi, darò prove evidenti,
che del mio cor l'insidator molesto è sol
Neron; ma poi, e che farai, Signor?

Poppea:
Do you still doubt me? Trust me, and if
you like. I will prove to you that he who
lays unwelcome siege to my heart is Nero
alone. What will you do then, my lord?

Claudio:
Le tue vendette.

Claudius:
Avenge you!

Poppea:
Ciò mi prometti?

Poppea:
You promise me?

Claudio:
Giuro!

Claudius:
I swear it!

Poppea:
E tanto io da te spero!
Vedrai se ho il cor mendace o pur sincero.
Vieni meco, Signore, e qui t'arresta.

Poppea:
Exactly as I hoped!
You will see if I am honest or deceitful.
Come this way, my lord, and stand there.

Poppea leads Claudius within the central door, and then goes over to Nero.

Nerone:
(Claudio partì?)

Nero:
(Has Claudius left?)

Ottone:
(Quanto il tardar molesta!)

Otho:
(This waiting is unbearable!)

Poppea:
Nerone, dove sei?

Poppea:
Nero, where are you?

Nerone:
Son qui, mia vita.

Nero:
I'm here, my dear.

Claudio:
Temerario, insolente!

Claudius:
You presumptuous, impudent lout!

Nerone:
(Oh ciel, aita!)

Nero:
(Heaven help me!)

Claudio:
Sin nella reggia istessa, baldanzoso garzòn,
osi impudico alle vergini eccelse usar
gl'insulti e ardito?

Claudius:
Within the very palace itself, you arrogant
boy, you brazenly and indecently
insult the virtue of blameless maidens?

Nerone:
Odi, Signor!

Nero:
Hear me, my lord!

Claudio:
Taci!

Claudius:
Be quiet!

Poppea:
(Contenta son.)

Poppea:
(Well and good.)

Ottone:
(Giubila, o core!)

Otho:
(Rejoice, my heart!)

Claudio:
Parti da mia presenza, né ardisci mai di
comparirmi inante!

Claudius:
Leave my presence, and never dare to
appear before me again!

As Nero departs, Poppea rebukes him.

Poppea:
(Và ad Agrippina, e di'…)

Poppea: *(aside, to Nero)*
Go to Agrippina, and tell her...)

Nerone:
(Ahi! crudo fato!)

Nero:
(Alas, cruel fate!)

Poppea:
(…che, chi cerca ingannar, resta
ingannato.)

Poppea:
… that he who seeks to deceive shall be
deceived.)

Nerone:
(Quale ad Augusto cor empia s'aspetta,
Agrippina saprà far la vendetta.)

Nero: *(departing)*
(From her imperial spirit, await Agrippina.
She knows how to exact revenge.)

Claudio, Poppea, Otho remains hidden.

Poppea:
Ora, Claudio, che dici?

Poppea:
Now Claudius, what do you say?

Claudio:
Io son convinto.

Claudius:
I am convinced.

Poppea:
Il mio sincero cor ora discopri.
(Per togliermi da Claudio arte s'adopri)
Mà d'Agrippina tutte, lassa! parmi veder
sciolte le furie, Pien di sdegno Nerone
alla madre ricorre; ah, che mi veggo
circondata d'affanni!

Poppea:
Now the sincerity of my heart is revealed.
(I must be cunning to rid myself of Claudius.)
But Agrippina, alas, will let loose all her
furies.
Nero will run to his mother in a tempest.
Ah, I see myself beset by problems!

Claudio:
Nulla, oh cara, temer, asciuga il ciglio!

Claudius:
Fear nothing, my dear; dry those eyes.

Poppea:
Io sono per tuo amor in gran periglio,
or non è tempo, oh Augusto;
la mia mente confusa non distingue gioire.
Verrà tosto Agrippina; ahi che martire!

Poppea:
Your love has placed me in great danger.
Not now, Caesar, my mind is disturbed
and bent on anything but pleasure.
Agrippina will soon be here: what torture!

Claudio:
No, non verrà!

Claudius:
No, she shall not come.

Poppea:
Deh, parti! Nulla otterrai da me!

Poppea:
Leave! You shall obtain nothing from me.

Claudio:
Sempre infelice sarà dunque il mio amor?

Claudius:
Then shall my love be forever unhappy?

Poppea:
Della consorte tempra prima il rigore;
fà che sicura io sia dal suo furore;
allor chiedi, e saprai qual sia il mio core.

Poppea:
First moderate the anger of your consort.
Make me safe from her fury: then ask,
and you shall know what my heart feels.

Claudio:
Io di Roma il Giove sono né v'è già chi
meco imperi.
Van ramminghi al piè del trono, dov'io
son, gl'altrui pensieri.

Claudius: *(before departing)*
I am the Jupiter of Rome, and share my
power with no one.
Around the foot of my throne dance the
ambitions of others.

Poppea looks around to confirm that Claudius has departed.

Poppea:
Pur alfin se n'andò.
Deh, quanto alletta il cor dolce vendetta!
Claudio partì; dubbio non v'è d'inganno;
volo a trar il mio ben dal lungo affanno.

Poppea:
At last he's left!
How sweet revenge delights the heart!
Claudius has gone. The trick worked.
Now to free my darling from his vigil.

Esci, o mia vita, esci dal duolo,
ch'a dar consolo vengo al tuo cor!
Per darti vita, caro, t'attendo;
vieni correndo, mio dolce amor!

Get out my life; get out of the duel.
I give consolation. I come to your heart!
To give you life, dear, I am waiting for
you; come running, my sweet love!

Poppea opens the curtain where Otho is hiding.

Oh Ottone, che dici?
Vedi come schernito restò Nerone,
e come d'Agrippina si vendicò il mio cor;
vedi, ch'io sprezzo il regnator del mondo,
e per te sol, mio bene, vivo involta d'amor
tra le catene.

Well, Otho. what do you say?
You see Nero was made a fool of, and my
heart have its revenge on Agrippina.
You see that I scorn the ruler of the world,
and for you alone, my darling,
I live enveloped in love's fetters.

Ottone:
Catene fortunate, se ci stringono insieme,
e in nodi eterni per la mano d'amore
formano di due cori un solo core.

Poppea:
Sperar dunque poss'io da te fede sincera?

Ottone:
Pria che mancarti, oh bella, mille volte
morrò.

Poppea:
Ciò mi prometti?

Ottone:
E unisco alle promesse il giuramento;
scagli fulmini il ciel, cara, se mento.

Poppea:
Ma se Claudio…?

Ottone:
Nol curo.

Poppea:
Agrippina, Neron?

Ottone:
Io gli disprezzo.

Poppea:
Lo splendore del soglio?

Ottone:
Pur ch'io ti stringa al sen, tutto
abbandono.

Poppea:
A te, mio ben, offro me stessa in dono.

Ottone:
Purch'io stringa al sen, mio caro dolce
ben, io son contento.
Senza di te, mio cor, è tutto in me dolor,
tutto è tormento.

Otho:
Most fortunate fetters, that bind us
together in eternal knots which, touched
by love's hand, make of two hearts one.

Poppea:
Can I place my trust in your sincere
faithfulness?

Otho:
I shall die a thousand times, beloved,
before failing you.

Poppea:
You promise?

Otho:
And I promise an oath: may heaven rain
down thunderbolts upon me, if I lie.

Poppea:
But if Claudius …?

Otho:
I do not care.

Poppea:
Agrippina, Nero?

Otho:
I despise them.

Poppea:
The splendors of the throne?

Otho:
So long as I may clasp you to my breast,
I shall give up all of my will.

Poppea:
My love, I am entirely yours.

Otho: *(before departing)*
So long as I may clasp you to my breast,
my love, I am happy.
But without you, my heart,
I am nothing but pain and torment.

Poppea:
Piega pur del mio cor nell dolce nido
placido le tue piume, oh mio Cupido!

Bel piacere è godere fido amor!
Questo fà contento il cor!
Di belezza non s'apprezza lo splendor,
se non vien d'un fido cor!

Agrippina:
Cotanto osò Poppea?

Nerone:
Come narrai, m'allettò, m'invitò,
m'accolse, e poi a Cesare scoprirmi!
Egli freme, essa ride ed io tremante a te
ricorro, oh madre, per sottrarmi allo
sdegno di Claudio, e al mio periglio.
Egl'è sposo, tu madre ed io son figlio.

Agrippina:
Ah! mal cauto Nerone, all'or ch'io tutti
adopro per innalzarti al trono arti ed
inganni, tu seguace d'un cieco e folle amor
al precipizio corri?

Nerone:
È vero, errai; ma l'arti tue e gl'inganni
già discoprì Poppea, "Vanne" ella disse,
"ad Agrippina, e dille che chi cerca
ingannar, resta ingannato."

Agrippina:
Non perciò tutta ancora languisce la mia
speme.
Figlio, smorza nel seno la fiamma indegna!
Guarda qual nemica Poppea! Del tuo pensiero
degno oggetto non sia, ch'il solo impero.

Nerone:
Come nube che fugge dal vento
abbandono sdegnato quel volto.
Il mio foco nel seno già spento, di
quest'alma già il laccio è disciolto.

Pallante:
Evvi donna più empia?

Poppea:
Fold your ardor in my nest, yes, my
sweet Cupid!

Pleasure is the joy of sincere love!
That makes the heart happy!
Beauty can not be appreciated if it does
not come from a trusting heart!

Agrippina: *(meeting with Nero)*
Poppea dared do this?

Nero:
As I said. I was enticed, invited, welcomed,
and then betrayed to Claudius!
He was furious, she laughed, and I was
terrified. I ran to you, mother, to save me
from Claudius. He is your husband, you
my mother, and I your son.

Agrippina:
Ah! Rash Nero, just when I am employing
every possible stratagem to raise you to
the throne, you pursue a blind and foolish
love to the very edge of doom?

Nero:
True! I erred. But Poppea has uncovered
your stratagems and spoils. "Go" - she
said - "to Agrippina, and tell her that he
who deceives shall be deceived."

Agrippina:
Yet not on that account shall my hope
quite wither away.
My son, smother this base passion within
your breast. See Poppea as an enemy.
Think of no object worthy but empire alone.

Nero:
As a cloud flies from the wind,
I renounce her despised face.
The fire is now cold within my breast,
my heart has already loosed its chain.

Pallas:
Was ever a woman more wicked?

Narciso:
E qual rigore nutrir si può maggior
dentro ad un core? E che farem?

Narcissus:
What greater coldness could be nurtured
within a heart? What shall we do?

Pallante:
È d'uopo tutto a Claudio scoprir;
egl'ha per noi bontà ch'ogn'altra eccede;
si prevenga l'accusa, e d'Augusta l'error a
noi sia scusa.

Pallas:
Reveal all to Claudius! His goodwill
towards us exceeds what he bears to all
others. Let the accusation be forestalled,
and Agrippina excuse what we have done

Narciso:
In così gran periglio approvo il tuo
consiglio.

Narcissus:
In our great danger your advice seems
good to me.

Pallante:
Mà qui sen vien Augusto.

Pallas:
But here comes Caesar.

Narciso:
Amico, è questo il tempo, ch'adopri del
tuo dir l'arte feconda.

Narcissus:
This is a favorable moment to advance the
plan you suggested.

Pallante:
Lascia la cura a me; tu mi seconda.

Pallas:
Leave it to me, but back me up.

Claudio:
Agrippina, Nerone, Otton, Poppea,
nell'accusa discordi, conturban la mia
quiete, né so chi dice il ver, o chi mentisca;
perché provi chi è reo giusto rigore.

Claudius:
Agrippina, Nero, Otho and Poppea,
trouble me by accusing one another. I
know not who tells the truth, and who
lies so as to punish the guilty one.

Pallante:
Alle tue reggie piante, Signor, ecco
prostrato l'infelice Pallante.

Pallas:
At your imperial feet, sir,
behold the unhappy Pallas falls.

Narciso:
Per difender sua vita chiede da te Narciso,
Augusto, aita!

Narcissus:
To save his life, Caesar,
Narcissus asks for your help.

Claudio:
Miei fidi, e qual insidia contro voi si
tenta? Che fia? Scoprite!

Claudius:
My loyal friends, whatever may be the
conspiracy plotted against you, reveal it!

Pallante:
Umile per la nostra discolpa porgo,
Signor, l'accusa; perché sol d'Agrippina
la minaccia è ver noi d'alta ruina.

Pallas:
Meekly, and via exculpation, my lord, I
render the accusation; from Agrippina
alone comes the threat of utter ruin.

Claudio:
Per qual cagion?

Claudius:
How is that?

Pallante:
Sul trono, pria che giungesti in Roma,
qual Cesare ella fè sieder Nerone;
di nostr'opra si valse, mà chi opra per
inganno è senza colpa.

Pallas:
Before you reached Rome, she placed
Nero as Caesar on the throne.
She availed herself of our labors, but being
tricked should not be considered a fault.

Narciso:
Di tua morte il supposto è a noi discolpa.

Narcissus:
Our belief that you had died is our excuse.

Claudio:
Agrippina tant'osa? Ora confermo ciò che
disse Poppea;
entro la reggia son domestici occulti i miei
nemici;
la tema al cor giusto sospetto infonde,
e fra tante vicende ei si confonde.
Voi siete fidi, il braccio mio possente di
scudo a voi sarà; non più timore!

Claudius:
Agrippina dared do this? What Poppea
told me is therefore confirmed.
Within the very palace lie my secret
enemies;
yet I fear and suspect. and in the midst of
confusion they are confounded.
You are loyal men, and my mighty arm
shall be your shield. Fear no more!

Agrippina:
Adorato mio sposo, è questo il giorno,
in cui di tue promesse attendo il fine.
A Nerone l'alloro oggi destina,
e ai tuoi piedi prostrato ogni rubel vedrai.

Agrippina:
My adored husband, now is the moment
when I await your promises.
Let Nero be crowned this very day, and
every rebel will prostrate at your feet.

Claudio:
Non già, Agrippina.

Claudius:
Not so fast, Agrippina.

Agrippina:
(Sdegnoso mi favella?)
Già il periglio t'è noto,
e il rimedio sicuro è a te palese;
Signor, che tardi più?
Pronto ripara l'imminente ruina,
i nemici reprimi!

Agrippina:
(He is angry with me.)
Your danger is now known to you,
and its remedy is obvious.
My lord, why delay further?
Forthwith avoid imminent ruin,
and stop your enemies!

Claudio:
E Agrippina?

Claudius:
And Agrippina?

Agrippina:
(Dissimular non giova. Qui è narciso e
Pallante;
superi un pronto ardir ogni riguardo!)

Agrippina:
(It's useless to pretend,
with Narcissus and Pallas present:
I shall have to be brazen!)

Pallante, Narciso:
(Come volge ver me sdegnosa il guardo!)

Agrippina:
Dal tuo dir già suppongo l'arti accorte
de' miei, de' tuoi nemici.
Parla, parla, discopri
qual dello sdegno tuo sia la cagione.

Claudio:
Cesare lo dirà; lo sà Nerone.

Agrippina:
Ah! Claudio, ora m'avveggo,
ch'ancora il ben oprar tal'ora è colpa.

Narciso:
(Or che dirà?)

Pallante:
(Sentiam la sua discolpa.)

Claudio:
Tu chiami ben oprar, tentar audace
d'usurparmi l'impero e, colto
il tempo della mia lontananza,
por Nerone sul trono?
Qual scusa addur potrai, che ti ricopra?

Agrippina:
Le scuse non adopra un cor sincero.
Quel che dici, Signor, il tutto è vero.

Claudio:
L'error confessi, ardita?

Agrippina:
Error non è il salvarti e trono e vita!
Godo che qui presenti sian Narciso e
Pallante.

Narciso:
(Che fermezza ha costei!)

Pallante:
(Che cor costante!)

Pallas, Narcissus:
(What poison from Agrippina!)

Agrippina:
From your tone I suspect malicious acts
from you and my enemies.
Speak, then, speak, what is the reason for
your anger?

Claudius:
Caesar will speak and Nero shall know.

Agrippina:
Ah! Claudius, I realize now that a good
deed can sometimes be a crime.

Narcissus:
(What will she say now?)

Pallas:
(Let's hear her excuse.)

Claudius:
You call it a brazen good deed to attempt
to usurp my throne, and, seizing the
opportunity of my absence, to set Nero
upon it?
How can you justify your behavior?

Agrippina:
A sincere heart makes no excuses.
What you say, my lord, is perfectly true.

Claudius:
You confess your error, audacious woman?

Agrippina:
To save your throne and your life was no
error. How happy I am that Narcissus and
Pallas are here.

Narcissus:
(What steady nerves!)

Pallas:
(How cool she is!)

Agrippina:
Precorse lode al ciel, fama bugiarda,
che nel fatal naufragio tua vita ancor
perisse.
Già le milizie, il popolo, il senato
rivolta al successor avean la mente.

Viddi ch'un cor altiero alzato al soglio,
con quella novità che sempre piace,
formava un gran nemico alla tua pace;
per riparare al danno, acclamar feci
il figlio; egli al soglio salì; ma ciò fu solo
per conservarlo a te, caro mio sposo!
Nel diffender tua vita, per mantenerti in
trono,
io la nemica, io la rubella sono?

Agrippina:
It was falsely (thank heaven!) rumored
abroad that in the fatal shipwreck
your very life had perished.
The army, the people and the Senate were
all ready to rebel for your successor.

I foresaw that a proud spirit, raised to the
throne, would do great damage to our
interests.
To ward off the danger I had my son
proclaimed. He ascended the throne - but
solely to preserve it for you, my dear
husband!
In defending your life, and maintaining
your throne, am I then an enemy, a rebel?

Pallante:
(Quanto è scaltra costei!)

Pallas:
(How crafty she is!)

Narciso:
(Quanto ella è accorta!)

Narcissus:
(How cunning!)

Agrippina:
E Pallante e Narciso del mio oprar
facciano fede.
Forse voi non richiesi per assister
all'opra?
Dite pure se all'avviso, ch'il ciel Claudio
salvò, Nerone umile non discese dal
soglio?
S'egli, unito a' miei voti, non fè di tutta
Roma i "viva" risuonar di Claudio al
nome?
Parli d'ogn'un di voi il cor sincero!

Agrippina:
Let Pallas and Narcissus bear witness to
my deeds.
Did I not ask you to help me in my task?
Say, then, whether upon the news
that Claudius's life was saved,
Nero did not humbly dismount the
throne,
and whether he, at one with my wishes,
did not cause the whole of Rome
to cheer at the very name of Claudius?
Let each of you speak frankly.

Claudio:
Voi che dite?

Claudius:
Well speak up!

Narciso, Pallante:
Signor, il tutto è vero.

Narcissus, Pallas:
My lord, it is perfectly true.

Agrippina:
E chi, fuorché il mio figlio,
una volta regnante,
dell'aura popolare fatto superbo,
ceduto avria lo scettro?

Agrippina:
And who but my own son,
having once reigned,
and made proud by popular approbation,
would have resigned the scepter?

Per difender tua vita, per mantenerti in
trono, io la nemica, io al rubella sono?

Claudio:
(Mi confonde Agrippina;
da istessi accusator ella è difesa!)

Narciso:
(Stupito son!)

Pallante:
(Della sua colpa ha merto!)

Claudio:
Di tua fè, del tuo amore, cara, son certo.

Agrippina:
Mà, oh Dio, certa io non son né di tua
fedeltà, né del tuo amore.
Penso che presso te fatta son rea,
perché il tuo cor ascolta...

Claudio:
E chi?

Agrippina:
Poppea. Duolmi sol, che l'inganno
a te non fia palese.

Claudio:
Scoprilo pur.

Agrippina:
Costei, vagheggiata d'Ottone...

Claudio:
Agrippina, t'inganni; egli è Nerone.
Olà vengano tosto Otton, Neron, Poppea!

Agrippina:
Vedrai s'io ti tradisco, e s'ella è rea!
(Ciò, che deve avvenire, io già preveggo.)

Claudio:
Fra tanti avvenimenti saprò chi è
contumace.
Vò che viva nei cor riposo e pace.

In defending your very life, in maintaining
your throne, am I the enemy, a rebel?

Claudius:
(Agrippina has outwitted me; her own
accusers defend her!)

Narcissus:
(I am amazed!)

Pallas:
(Her own crime brings her a reward!)

Claudius:
Of your loyalty and love, I have no doubt.

Agrippina:
But, dear god, I am certain neither of your
loyalty, nor your love.
I believe that I am guilty in your eyes
because your heart listens to...

Claudius:
To whom?

Agrippina:
Poppea. It pains me only that her deceit
is not apparent to you.

Claudius:
Then reveal it.

Agrippina:
This woman, desired by Otho...

Claudius:
Agrippina, you are deceived: it was Nero.
Send for Otho, Nero and Poppea!

Agrippina:
You will see if I lie or she is guilty.
(I have already foreseen the outcome.)

Claudius:
With such turns of events I must know
who resists my authority. I want peace
and tranquillity to reign in our hearts.

Agrippina:
Se vuoi pace, oh volto amato, l'odio reo
fuga da te!
Guarda in me, nume adorato, il mio amore
e la mia fè.

(Ecco la mia rivale)

Poppea:
(Ecco quel empia cagion di doglia ria.)

Nerone:
(Che mai sarà di me?)

Ottone:
(Cieli, che fia?)

Claudio:
Vedi, Agrippina, il figlio, quell'ardito
garzon, che nella reggia delle vergini
eccelse tenta offender l'onor.

Agrippina:
T'inganni, Augusto.

Claudio:
Nò, non m'inganno, nò, l'erro confessa.
Di Poppea nelle stanze non ti trovai
nascosto?

Agrippina:
Cieli, che sento mai?

Nerone:
(Parlar non oso.)

Claudio:
Accusa col silenzio il suo delitto.
Tu l'attesta, oh Poppea, con cor sincero!

Poppea:
Lo vedesti, Signor, purtroppo è vero.

Agrippina:
(L'arte ancor di costei sarà ingannata)

Agrippina:
If you want peace, my handsome lover,
then chase vile hatred from you!
See in me, my adored one, love and
loyalty.

(Here comes my hated rival.)

Poppea:
(Here is the shameless cause of much
unhappiness.)

Nero:
(Whatever will become of me?)

Otho:
(Heavens, what will happen?)

Claudius:
See, Agrippina, your son, that unruly boy,
who dares to insult the honor of blameless
maidens in the palace itself.

Agrippina:
You are deceived, Caesar.

Claudius:
No, I am not deceived. He confesses error.
Did I not find you hidden in Poppea's
apartments?

Agrippina:
Heavens, what do I hear?

Nero:
(I'd better say nothing.)

Claudius:
His silence accuses him.
You can witness this, Poppea, sincerely.

Poppea:
As you saw, my lord, it is all too true.

Agrippina:
(Her schemes shall still be thwarted.)

Ottone:
(Come accorta Poppea s'è vendicata!)

Otho:
(How cleverly Poppea had her revenge!)

Claudio:
Vuo', che colpa palese palese abbia l'emenda.

Claudius:
Such a blatant crime should have exemplary correction.

Agrippina:
(Spera ancora il mio cor.)

Agrippina:
(My heart is still hopeful.)

Poppea:
(Oh quanto io godo!)

Poppea:
(How I am enjoying this!)

Claudio:
Di Nerone e Poppea stringa dolce Imeneo l'illustre nodo!

Claudius:
Let sweet Hymen's illustrious knot join Nero and Poppea!

Poppea:
(Che sento mai?)

Poppea:
(What is this?)

Agrippina:
(Ch'intendo?)

Agrippina:
(What do I hear?)

Nerone:
A tue grazie, Signor, vinto mi rendo.

Nero:
Sir, your graciousness conquers me.

Ottone:
Ecco prostrato, oh Augusto, quell'Ottone infelice!

Otho:
Behold, o Caesar, Otho is prostrate with grief!

Claudio:
Ormai t'accheta! Ebbi delle tue colpe il disinganno;
ti promisi l'alloro, Cesare tu sarai.

Claudius:
Henceforth be appeased, I stand corrected as to your guilt! I promised you the laurel wreath, and Caesar you shall be.

Agrippina:
(Sento e non moro!)

Agrippina:
(I hear this and do not die!)

Ottone:
Io l'allora rifiuto, di regnar non mi curo,
e solo apprezzo la mia cara Poppea.
Se di darti la vita ebbi la sorte,
nel togliermi il mio ben tu mi dai morte.

Otho:
I refuse the laurel, for I care not for power; all I prize is Poppea. If fate ordained that I saved your life, depriving me of my beloved, brings me death.

Agrippina:
Ora vedi, chi sia, che ha l'alma rea,
s'è Nerone o s'è otton ch'ama Poppea!

Agrippina:
Now see who has the blackest soul. Is it Nero or Otho that loves Poppea!

Claudio:
E tu, neron, che dici?

Nerone:
Ubbidiente io son alle tue voglie; ma
doppio mio castigo è il togliermi l'impero
e darmi moglie.

Poppea:
E con me non si parla? Scettri, regni ed
imperi abbia Nerone; d'altri mai non sarò,
fuorche d'Ottone.

Claudio:
Io dei vostri desir volli far prova.

Se lasci per l'allor volto divino,
a Ottone se sprezzi per amor di Roma il
trono, ai posteri sarete dell'amor, del
regnar eroi ben degni.

Cesare fia Neron, tu stringi, Ottone,
la tua Poppea costante!
(Ho sciolto il cor, s'ell'è d'un altro
amante)

Nerone, Poppea:
Felice son.

Ottone:
Più il duol non mi tormenta.

Agrippina:
(Or che regna Neron, moro contenta)

Claudio:
Habbian termine gl'odi, e Roma
applauda a questo dì bramato,
che ogni un rende contento e fortunato.

Dell'Augusto mio genio, per gli eccelsi
sponsali d'Ottone e di Poppea,
Pronuba Giuno già s'invitò nell'apparato
illustre. Ella ormai scenda, e Roma
intrecci di Neron lauri alla chioma.

Claudius: *(to Nero)*
And you Nero, what do you say?

Nero:
I will abide by your wishes,
but my punishment is a double one:
to be deprived of empire, and a wife.

Poppea:
And you have nothing to say to me?
Let Nero have all the scepters, power and
empires that he will, I shall be nothing
else but belong to Otho.

Claudius:
I wish to make a trial of your desires.
(to Nero)
If you give up beauty for the laurel
wreath, if you disdain Rome itself for
love, to posterity, you shall be worthy
heroes of love, and of empire.

Let Nero be Caesar, while you, Otho,
shall clasp your faithful Poppea!
(My heart is freed, if she is another's
lover.)

Nero, Poppea:
What happiness!

Otho:
Grief no longer torments me.

Agrippina:
(Now, Nero is emperor, I can die happy.)

Claudius:
Let hatred be at an end,
and let Rome greet the longed-for day,
that brings contentment and good fortune.

At Caesar's behest, to honor this
auspicious wedding of the lovely Poppea,
Juno, goddess of marriage shall attend.
Now she descends, and let Rome
entwine the laurel to Nero's brow.

Juno descends with her retinue.

Coro:
Lieto il Tebro increspi l'onda
sotto ai rai del nuovo allor,
e festeggi su la sponda
pien di gioja il Dio d'amor!

Chorus:
May the happy Tiber curl its waves
beneath the new laurel's glitter,
and may the god of love
transport himself gaily to the shore!

Giunone:
D'Otton e di Poppea sul grande innesto
Scende Giuno dal cielo a sparger gigli.
E nel talamo eccelso io lieta appresto,
vassalli a Claudio e all' alta Roma i figli.

Juno:
To celebrate the joining of Otho and
Poppea, Juno descends from heaven to
scatter lilies, and from the bridal bed the
happy goddess expects new vassals for
Claudius, new sons for honored Rome.

V'accendano le tede i raggi delle stelle.
Esse per tanta fede già splendono più
belle.

The starlight kindles our torches,
which shine the more brilliantly
in honor of such beauty.

A dance of Juno — goddess of love and marriage.

END of OPERA

DICTIONARY OF OPERA AND MUSICAL TERMS

Accelerando - Play the music faster, but gradually.

Adagio - At slow or gliding tempo, not as slow as Largo, but not as fast as Andante.

Agitato - Restless or agitated.

Allegro - At a brisk or lively tempo, faster than Andante but not as fast as Presto.

Andante - A moderately slow, easy-going tempo.

Appoggiatura - An extra or embellishing note preceding a main melodic note or tone. Usually written as a note of smaller size, it shares the time value of the main note.

Arabesque - Flourishes or fancy patterns usually applying to vocal virtuosity.

Aria - A solo song usually structured in a formal pattern. Arias generally convey reflective and introspective thoughts rather than descriptive action.

Arietta - A shortened form of aria.

Arioso - A musical passage or composition having a mixture of free recitative and metrical song.

Arpeggio - Producing the tones of a chord in succession but not simultaneously.

Atonal - Music that is not anchored in traditional musical tonality; it uses the chromatic scale impartially, does not use the diatonic scale and has no keynote or tonal center.

Ballad Opera - 18th century English opera consisting of spoken dialogue and music derived from popular ballad and folksong sources. The most famous is *The Beggar's Opera* which was a satire of the Italian opera seria.

Bar - A vertical line across the stave that divides the music into units.

Baritone - A male singing voice ranging between the bass and tenor.

Baroque - A style of artistic expression prevalent in the 17th century that is marked generally by the use of complex forms, bold ornamentation, and florid decoration. The Baroque period extends from approximately 1600 to 1750 and includes the works of the original creators of modern opera, the Camerata, as well as the later works by Bach and Handel.

Bass - The lowest male voices, usually divided into categories such as:

> **Basso buffo** - A bass voice that specializes in comic roles like Dr. Bartolo in Rossini's *The Barber of Seville*.

> **Basso cantante** - A bass voice that demonstrates melodic singing quality rather than comic or tragic: King Philip in Verdi's *Don Carlos*.

> **Basso profundo** - the deepest, most profound, or most dramatic of bass voices: Sarastro in Mozart's *The Magic Flute.*

Bel canto - Literally "beautiful singing." It originated in Italian opera of the 17th and 18th centuries and stressed beautiful tones produced with ease, clarity, purity, evenness, together with an agile vocal technique and virtuosity. Bel canto flourished in the first half of the 19th century in the works of Rossini, Bellini, and Donizetti.

Cabaletta - Typically a lively bravura extension of an aria or duet that creates a climax. The term is derived from the Italian word "cavallo," or horse: it metaphorically describes a horse galloping to the finish line.

Cadenza - A flourish or brilliant part of an aria commonly inserted just before a finale.

Camerata - A gathering of Florentine writers and musicians between 1590 and 1600 who attempted to recreate what they believed was the ancient Greek theatrical synthesis of drama, music, and stage spectacle; their experimentation led to the creation of the early structural forms of modern opera.

Cantabile - An expression indication urging the singer to sing sweetly.

Cantata - A choral piece generally containing Scriptural narrative texts: Bach Cantatas.

Cantilena - A lyrical melodic line meant to be played or sung "cantabile," or with sweetness and expression.

Canzone - A short, lyrical operatic song usually containing no narrative association with the drama but rather simply reflecting the character's state of mind: Cherubino's "Voi che sapete" in Mozart's *The Marriage of Figaro.* Shorter versions are called canzonettas.

Castrato - A young male singer who was surgically castrated to retain his treble voice.

Cavatina - A short aria popular in the 18th century without the da capo repeat section.

Classical Period - The period between the Baroque and Romantic periods. The Classical period is generally considered to have begun with the birth of Mozart (1756) and ended with Beethoven's death (1830). Stylistically, the music of the period stressed clarity, precision, and rigid structural forms.

Coda - A trailer or tailpiece added on by the composer after the music's natural conclusion.

Coloratura - Literally colored: it refers to a soprano singing in the bel canto tradition with great agility, virtuosity, embellishments and ornamentation: Joan Sutherland singing in Donizetti's *Lucia di Lammermoor.*

Commedia dell'arte - A popular form of dramatic presentation originating in Renaissance Italy in which highly stylized characters were involved in comic plots involving mistaken identities and misunderstandings. The standard characters were Harlequin and Colombine: The "play within a play" in Leoncavallo's *I Pagliacci.*

Comprimario - A singer portraying secondary character roles such as confidantes, servants, and messengers.

Continuo - A bass part (as for a keyboard or stringed instrument) that was used especially in baroque ensemble music; it consists of a succession of bass notes with figures that indicate the required chords. Also called *figured bass, thoroughbass.*

Contralto - The lowest female voice derived from "contra" against, and "alto" voice, a voice between the tenor and mezzo-soprano.

Countertenor, or male alto vocal range - A high male voice generally singing within the female high soprano ranges.

Counterpoint - The combination of one or more independent melodies added into a single harmonic texture in which each retains its linear character: polyphony. The most sophisticated form of counterpoint is the fugue form in which up to 6 to 8 voices are combined, each providing a variation on the basic theme but each retaining its relation to the whole.

Crescendo - A gradual increase in the volume of a musical passage.

Da capo - Literally "from the top": repeat. Early 17th century da capo arias were in the form of A B A, the last A section repeating the first A section.

Deus ex machina - Literally "god out of a machine." A dramatic technique in which a person or thing appears or is introduced suddenly and unexpectedly; it provides a contrived solution to an apparently insoluble dramatic difficulty.

Diatonic - Relating to a major or minor musical scale that comprises intervals of five whole steps and two half steps.

Diminuendo - Gradually getting softer, the opposite of crescendo.

Dissonance - A mingling of discordant sounds that do not harmonize within the diatonic scale.

Diva - Literally a "goddess"; generally refers to a female opera star who either possesses, or pretends to possess, great rank.

Dominant - The fifth tone of the diatonic scale: in the key of C, the dominant is G.

Dramma giocoso - Literally meaning amusing, or lighthearted. Like tragicomedy it represents an opera whose story combines both serious and comic elements: Mozart's *Don Giovanni.*

Falsetto - Literally a lighter or "false" voice; an artificially produced high singing voice that extends above the range of the full voice.

Fioritura - Literally "flower"; a flowering ornamentation or embellishment of the vocal line within an aria.

Forte, Fortissimo - Forte (*f*) means loud: mezzo forte (*mf*) is fairly loud; fortissimo (*ff*) even louder, and additional *fff*'s indicate greater degrees of loudness.

Glissando - A rapid sliding up or down the scale.

Grand Opera - An opera in which there is no spoken dialogue and the entire text is set to music, frequently treating serious and dramatic subjects. Grand Opera flourished in France in the 19th century (Meyerbeer) and most notably by Verdi (Aida): the genre is epic in scale and combines spectacle, large choruses, scenery, and huge orchestras.

Heldentenor - A tenor with a powerful dramatic voice who possesses brilliant top notes and vocal stamina. Heldentenors are well suited to heroic (Wagnerian) roles: Lauritz Melchoir in Wagner's *Tristan und Isolde*.

Imbroglio - Literally "Intrigue"; an operatic scene with chaos and confusion and appropriate diverse melodies and rhythms.

Largo or larghetto - Largo indicates a very slow tempo; Larghetto is slightly faster than Largo.

Legato - Literally "tied"; therefore, successive tones that are connected smoothly. Opposing Legato would be Marcato (strongly accented and punctuated) and Staccato (short and aggressive).

Leitmotif - A short musical passage attached to a person, thing, feeling, or idea that provides associations when it recurs or is recalled.

Libretto - Literally "little book"; the text of an opera. On Broadway, the text of songs is called "lyrics" but the spoken text in the play is called the "book."

Lied - A German song; the plural is "lieder." Originally German art songs of the 19th century.

Light opera, or operetta - Operas that contain comic elements but light romantic plots: Johann Strauss's *Die Fledermaus.*

Maestro - From the Italian "master": a term of respect to conductors, composers, directors, and great musicians.

Melodrama - Words spoken over music. Melodrama appears in Beethoven's *Fidelio* but flourished during the late 19th century in the operas of Massenet (*Manon*). Melodrama should not be confused with melodrama when it describes a work that is characterized by extravagant theatricality and by the predominance of plot and physical action over characterization.

Mezza voce - Literally "medium voice," or singing with medium or half volume; it is generally intended as a vocal means to intensify emotion.

Mezzo-soprano - A woman's voice with a range between that of the soprano and contralto.

Molto - Very. Molto agitato means very agitated.

Obbligato - An elaborate accompaniment to a solo or principal melody that is usually played by a single instrument.

Octave - A musical interval embracing eight diatonic degrees: therefore, from C to C is an octave.

Opera - Literally "a work"; a dramatic or comic play combining music.

Opera buffa - Italian comic opera that flourished during the bel canto era. Buffo characters were usually basses singing patter songs: Dr. Bartolo in Rossini's *The Barber of Seville,* and Dr. Dulcamara in Donizetti's *The Elixir of Love.*

Opéra comique - A French opera characterized by spoken dialogue interspersed between the arias and ensemble numbers, as opposed to Grand Opera in which there is no spoken dialogue.

Operetta, or light opera - Operas that contain comic elements but tend to be more romantic: Strauss's *Die Fledermaus,* Offenbach's *La Périchole*, and Lehar's *The Merry Widow*. In operettas, there is usually much spoken dialogue, dancing, practical jokes, and mistaken identities.

Oratorio - A lengthy choral work, usually of a religious or philosophical nature and consisting chiefly of recitatives, arias, and choruses but in deference to its content, performed without action or scenery: Handel's *Messiah.*

Ornamentation - Extra embellishing notes—appoggiaturas, trills, roulades, or cadenzas—that enhance a melodic line.

Overture - The orchestral introduction to a musical dramatic work that frequently incorporates musical themes within the work.

Parlando - Literally "speaking"; the imitation of speech while singing, or singing that is almost speaking over the music. It is usually short and with minimal orchestral accompaniment.

Patter - Words rapidly and quickly delivered. Figaro's Largo in Rossini's *The Barber of Seville* is a patter song.

Pentatonic - A five-note scale, like the black notes within an octave on the piano.

Piano - Soft volume.

Pitch - The property of a musical tone that is determined by the frequency of the waves producing it.

Pizzicato - A passage played by plucking the strings instead of stroking the string with the bow.

Polyphony - Literally "many voices." A style of musical composition in which two or more independent melodies are juxtaposed in harmony; counterpoint.

Polytonal - The use of several tonal schemes simultaneously.

Portamento - A continuous gliding movement from one tone to another.

Prelude - An orchestral introduction to an act or the whole opera. An Overture can appear only at the beginning of an opera.

Presto, Prestissimo - Very fast and vigorous.

Prima Donna - The female star of an opera cast. Although the term was initially used to differentiate between the dramatic and vocal importance of a singer, today it generally describes the personality of a singer rather than her importance in the particular opera.

Prologue - A piece sung before the curtain goes up on the opera proper: Tonio's Prologue in Leoncavallo's *I Pagliacci*.

Quaver - An eighth note.

Range - The divisions of the voice: soprano, mezzo-soprano, contralto, tenor, baritone, and bass.

Recitative - A formal device that that advances the plot. It is usually a rhythmically free vocal style that imitates the natural inflections of speech; it represents the dialogue and narrative in operas and oratorios. Secco recitative is accompanied by harpsichord and sometimes with cello or continuo instruments and *accompagnato* indicates that the recitative is accompanied by the orchestra.

Ritornello - A short recurrent instrumental passage between elements of a vocal composition.

Romanza - A solo song that is usually sentimental; it is usually shorter and less complex than an aria and rarely deals with terror, rage, and anger.

Romantic Period - The period generally beginning with the raiding of the Bastille (1789) and the last revolutions and uprisings in Europe (1848). Romanticists generally found inspiration in nature and man. Beethoven's *Fidelio* (1805) is considered the first Romantic opera, followed by the works of Verdi and Wagner.

Roulade - A florid vocal embellishment sung to one syllable.

Rubato - Literally "robbed"; it is a fluctuation of tempo within a musical phrase, often against a rhythmically steady accompaniment.

Secco - The accompaniment for recitative played by the harpsichord and sometimes continuo instruments.

Semitone - A half-step, the smallest distance between two notes. In the key of C, the notes are E and F, and B and C.

Serial music - Music based on a series of tones in a chosen pattern without regard for traditional tonality.

Sforzando - Sudden loudness and force; it must stick out from the texture and provide a shock.

Singspiel - Early German musical drama employing spoken dialogue between songs: Mozart's *The Magic Flute*.

Soprano - The highest range of the female voice ranging from lyric (light and graceful quality) to dramatic (fuller and heavier in tone).

Sotto voce - Literally "below the voice"; sung softly between a whisper and a quiet conversational tone.

Soubrette - A soprano who sings supporting roles in comic opera: Adele in Strauss's *Die Fledermaus*, or Despina in Mozart's *Così fan tutte.*

Spinto - From the Italian "spingere" (to push); a soprano having lyric vocal qualities who "pushes" the voice to achieve heavier dramatic qualities.

Sprechstimme - Literally "speak voice." The singer half sings a note and half speaks; the declamation sounds like speaking but the duration of pitch makes it seem almost like singing.

Staccato - Short, clipped, rapid articulation; the opposite of the caressing effects of legato.

Stretto - A concluding passage performed in a quicker tempo to create a musical climax.

Strophe - Music repeated for each verse of an aria.

Syncopation - Shifting the beat forward or back from its usual place in the bar; it is a temporary displacement of the regular metrical accent in music caused typically by stressing the weak beat.

Supernumerary - A "super"; a performer with a non-singing role: "Spear-carrier."

Tempo - Time, or speed. The ranges are Largo for very slow to Presto for very fast.

Tenor - Highest natural male voice.

Tessitura - The general range of a melody or voice part; but specifically, the part of the register in which most of the tones of a melody or voice part lie.

Tonality - The organization of all the tones and harmonies of a piece of music in relation to a tonic (the first tone of its scale).

Tone Poem - An orchestral piece with a program; a script.

Tonic - The keynote of the key in which a piece is written. C is the tonic of C major.

Trill - Two adjacent notes rapidly and repeatedly alternated.

Tutti - All together.

Twelve tone - The 12 chromatic tones of the octave placed in a chosen fixed order and constituting with some permitted permutations and derivations the melodic and harmonic material of a serial musical piece. Each note of the chromatic scale is used as part of the melody before any other note gets repeated.

Verismo - Literally "truth"; the artistic use of contemporary everyday material in preference to the heroic or legendary in opera. A movement from the late 19th century: *Carmen.*

Vibrato - A "vibration"; a slightly tremulous effect imparted to vocal or instrumental tone for added warmth and expressiveness by slight and rapid variations in pitch.

Opera Journeys™ Mini Guide Series

Opera Journeys™ Libretto Series

Opera Classics Library™ Series

A History of Opera: Milestones and Metamorphoses

Puccini Companion

Verdi Companion

Mozart's Da Ponte Operas

Fifty Timeless Classics

PUCCINI COMPANION

Hard or Soft Cover editions

COMPLETE LIBRETTOS
Italian-English side-by-side

STORY NARRATIVE
with 100s of Music Highlight Examples

ANALYSIS AND COMMENTARY

Print or Ebook

A HISTORY of OPERA: MILESTONES and MEAMORPHOSES

432 pages, soft cover / 21 chapters
Over 250 music examples
featuring
• A comprehensive survey of milestones in opera history
• All periods are analyzed in depth:
Baroque, Classical, Romantic, Bel Canto, Opera Buffa,
German Romanticism, Wagner, music drama, Verismo,
plus analyses "Tristan Chord," atonalism, minimalism.

Print or Ebook

OPERA JOURNEYS' COLLECTION: 50 TIMELESS OPERA CLASSICS

816-page Soft Cover volume
A collection of fifty of the most popular operas
in the Opera Journeys Mini Guide Series,
each: Story Narrative and 100s of Music Examples,

PLUS insightful,in delpth Commentary and Analysis

Print ot Ebook

MOZART'S DA PONTE OPERAS
DON GIOVANNI; MARRIAGE FIGARO; COSI FAN TUTTE

348-page Soft or Hard Cover Edition

Mozart: Master of Musical Characterization;
Da Ponte: Ambassador of Italian Culture.
Featuring: Principal Characters, Brief Story Synopsis,
Story Narrative, Music Highlight Examples,
insightful in depth Commentary and Analysis,
Librettos with Italian-English translations side-by-side

ORDER: Opera Journeys' Web Site www.operajourneys.com

OPERA JOURNEYS LIBRETTO SERIES

Print or Ebook

New translations (side-by-side) with Music Highlight Examples

•Aida •The Barber of Seville •La Bohème
•Carmen •Cavalleria Rusticana •La Cenerentola
•Così fan tutte •Don Carlo •Don Giovanni
•La Fanciulla del West •Gianni Schicchi
•Lucia di Lammermoor •Madama Butterfly
•The Magic Flute •Manon Lescaut
•The Marriage of Figaro •A Masked Ball
•Otello •I Pagliacci •Rigoletto •La Rondine
•Salome Samson and Delilah •Suor Angelica
•Il Tabarro •Tosca •La Traviata •Il Trovatore •Turandot

OPERA JOURNEYS MINI GUIDE SERIES

Print or Ebook

featuring 125 titles

• *Brief Story Synopsis*

• *Principal Characters*

• *Story Narrative*

• *Music Highlight Examples*

• *Commentary and Analysis*

•The Abduction from the Seraglio •Adriana Lecouvreur •L'Africaine •Aida •Andrea Chénier •Anna Bolena •Ariadne auf Naxos •Armida •Attila •The Ballad of Baby Doe •The Barber of Seville •Duke Bluebeard's Castle •La Bohème •Boris Godunov •Candide •Capriccio •Carmen •Cavalleria Rusticana •Cendrillon •La Cenerentola •La Clemenza di Tito •Le Comte Ory •Così fan tutte •The Crucible •La Damnation de Faust •The Death of Klinghoffer •Doctor Atomic Don Carlo • Don Giovanni •Don Pasquale •La Donna del Lago •The Elixir of Love •Elektra •Ernani •Eugene Onegin •Falstaff •La Fanciulla del West •Faust •La Fille du Régiment •Fidelio •Die Fledermaus •The Flying Dutchman •Die Frau ohne Schatten •Der Freischütz •Gianni Schicchi •La Gioconda •Hamlet •Hansel and Gretel •Henry VIII •Iolanta •L'Italiana in Algeri •Les Huguenots •Iphigénie en Tauride •Julius Caesar •Lakmé •Lohengrin •Lucia di Lammermoor •Macbeth •Madama Butterfly •The Magic Flute •The Makropolis Case •Manon •Manon Lescaut •Maria Stuarda •The Marriage of Figaro •A Masked Ball •Die Meistersinger •The Mikado •Nabucco •Nixon in China •Norma •Of Mice and Men •Orfeo ed Euridice •Otello •I Pagliacci •Parsifal •The Pearl Fishers •Pelléas et Mélisande •Porgy and Bess •Prince Igor •I Puritani •The Queen of Spades •The Rake's Progress •The Rape of Lucretia •The Rhinegold •Rigoletto •The Ring of the Nibelung •Roberto Devereaux •Rodalinda •Roméo et Juliette •La Rondine •Der Rosenkavalier •Rusalka •Salome •Samson and Delilah •Show Boat •Siegfried •Simon Boccanegra •La Sonnambula •Suor Angelica •Susannah •Il Tabarro •The Tales of Hoffmann •Tannhäuser •Thaïs •Tosca •La Traviata •Tristan and Isolde •Il Trittico •Les Troyens •Il Trovatore •Turandot •Twilight of the Gods •The Valkyrie •Werther •West Side Story •Wozzeck

OPERA CLASSICS LIBRARY™
Opera Study Guides
WITH
Librettos
EDITED BY Burton D. Fisher

Available at
Amazon.com or Opera Journeys.com

Each *Opera Classic Library* edition features...

- *Principal Characters in the Opera*
- *Brief Story Synopsis*
- *Commentary and Analysis*
- *Story Narrative with Music Highlights*
- *Libretto - parallel, side-by-side translation*

"THE COLLECTION"

Adriana Lecouvreur	La Forza del Destino	Les Pecheurs de Perles
Aida	Gianni Schicchi	Porgy and Bess
Andrea Chénier	La Gioconda	I Puritani
Anna Bolena	Giulio Cesare	Das Rheingold
Attila	Gotterdämmerung	The Ring of the Nibelung
Un Ballo in Maschera	Hänsel and Gretel	Rigoletto
Il Barbiere di Siviglia	Idomeneo	Roberto Devereux
La Bohème	Lohengrin	Roméo et Juliette
Carmen	Lucia di Lammermoor	Der Rosenkavalier
Cavalleria Rusticana	Luisa Miller	Salome
Cendrillon	Lulu	Samson and Delilah
La Cenerentola	Macbeth	Semiramide
La Clemenza di Tito	Madama Butterfly	Siegfried
Les Contes d'Hoffmann	The Magic Flute	Simon Boccanegra
Così fan tutte	Manon	La Sonnambula
Don Carlo	Manon Lescaut	Suor Angelica
Don Giovanni	Maria Stuarda	Il Tabarro
La Donna del Lago	Mefistofele	Tannhäuser
Elektra	Die Meistersinger	Thaïs
L'Elisir d'Amore	Nabucco	Tosca
Ernani	Norma	La Traviata
Falstaff	Le Nozze di Figaro	Tristan und Isolde
La Fanciulla del West	Orfeo ed Euridice	Il Trovatore
Faust	Otello	Turandot
Fidelio	I Pagliacci	Die Walküre
La Fille de Règiment	Parsifal	Werther
Die Fliegende Holländer		Wozzeck

Made in the USA
San Bernardino, CA
15 August 2019